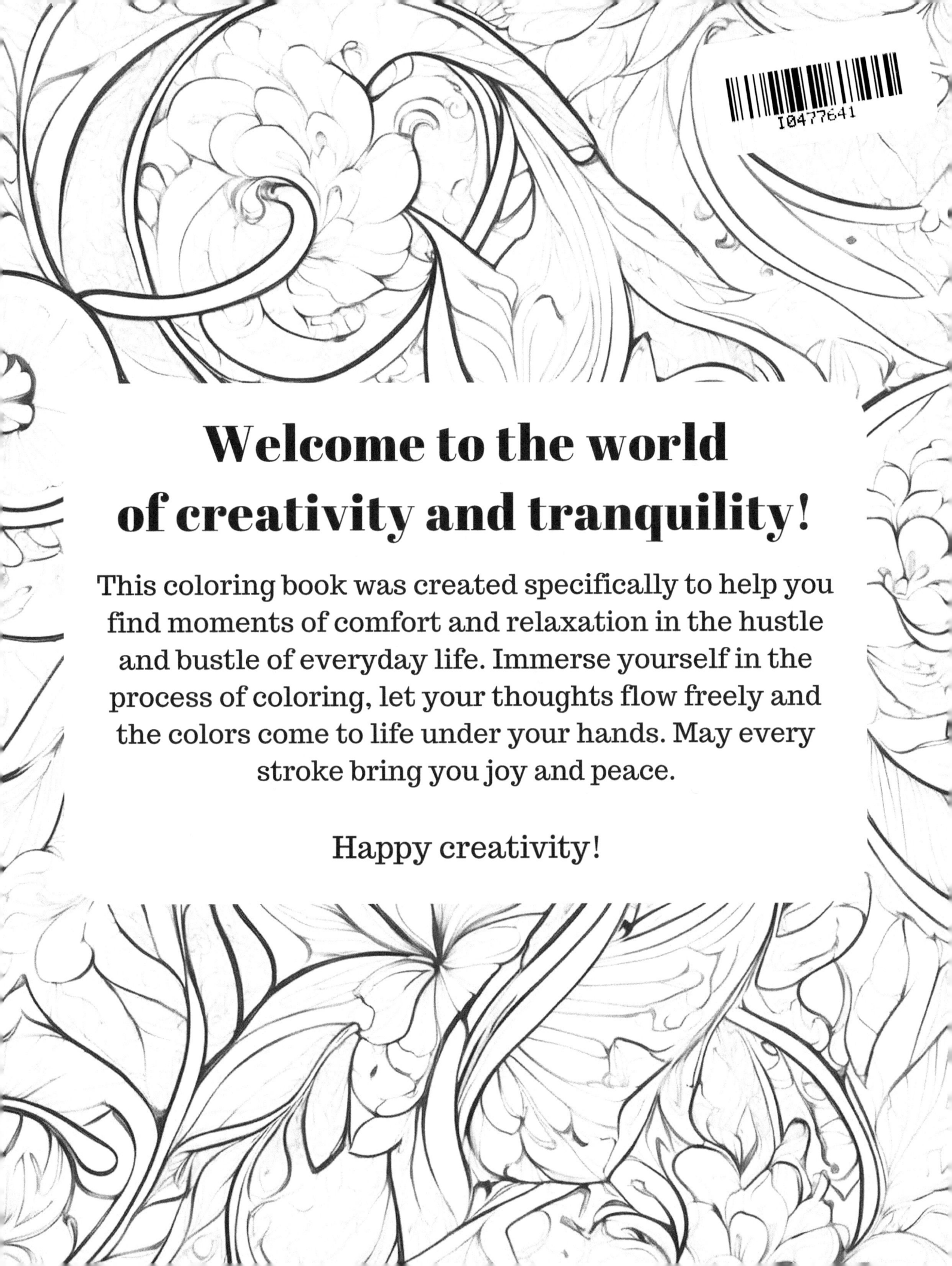

Welcome to the world of creativity and tranquility!

This coloring book was created specifically to help you find moments of comfort and relaxation in the hustle and bustle of everyday life. Immerse yourself in the process of coloring, let your thoughts flow freely and the colors come to life under your hands. May every stroke bring you joy and peace.

Happy creativity!

20+ FREE DIGITAL COLOURING PAGES

Thank you for choosing our book!

Visit the "Emiliya Wright Coloring" page on Facebook to download them now!

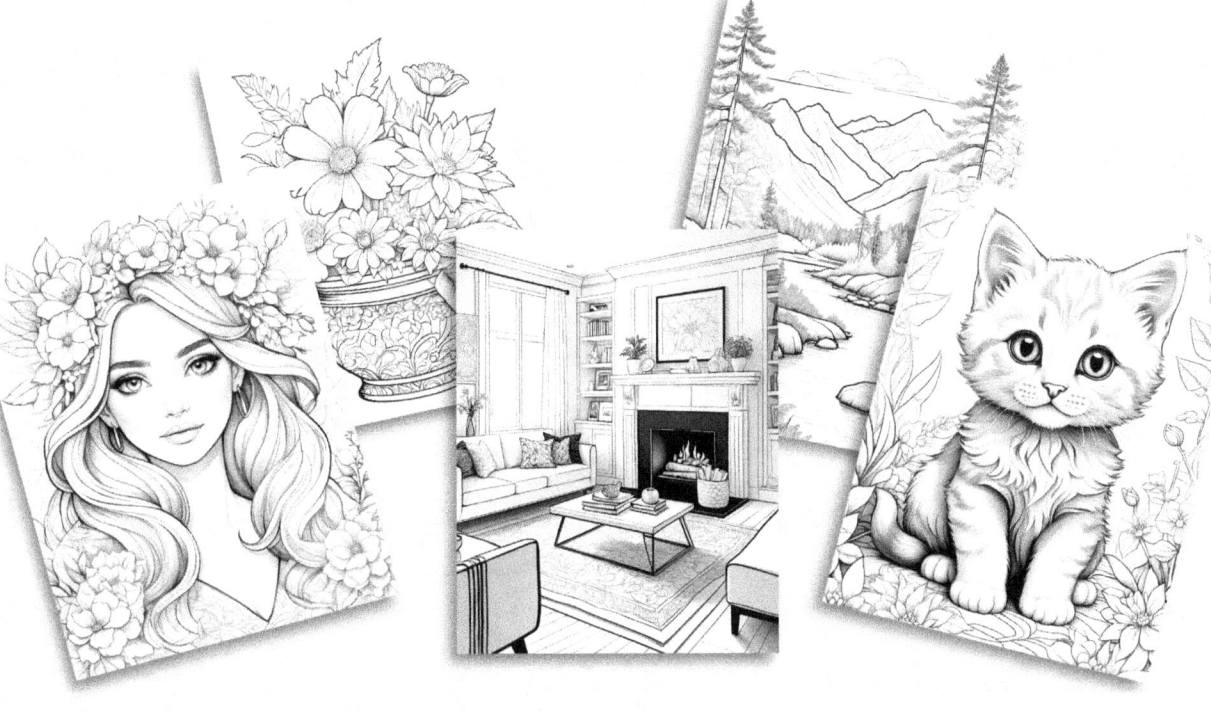

Follow our Facebook page to let your creativity shine.

Scan the QR code to follow the page:

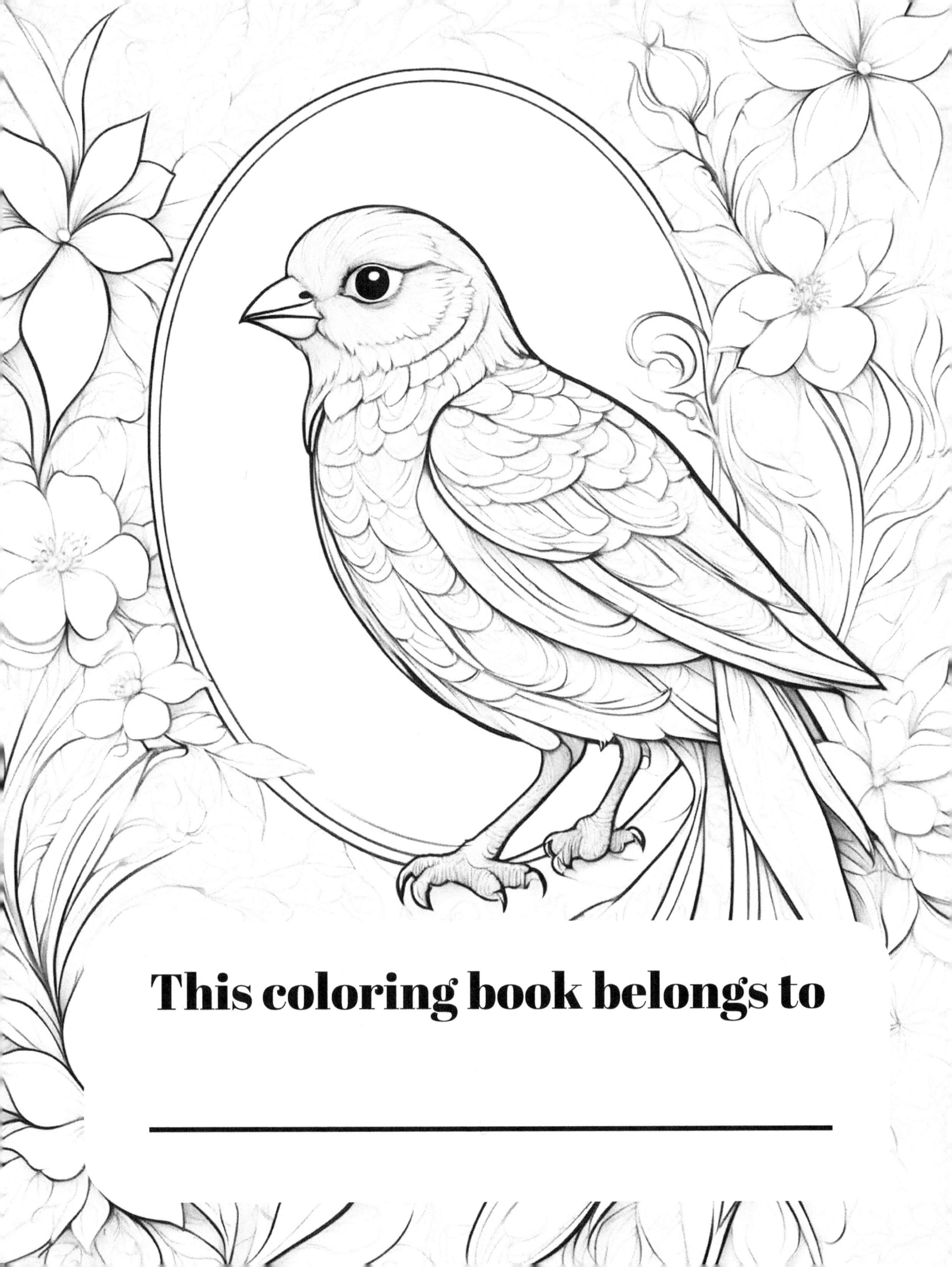

This coloring book belongs to

_____

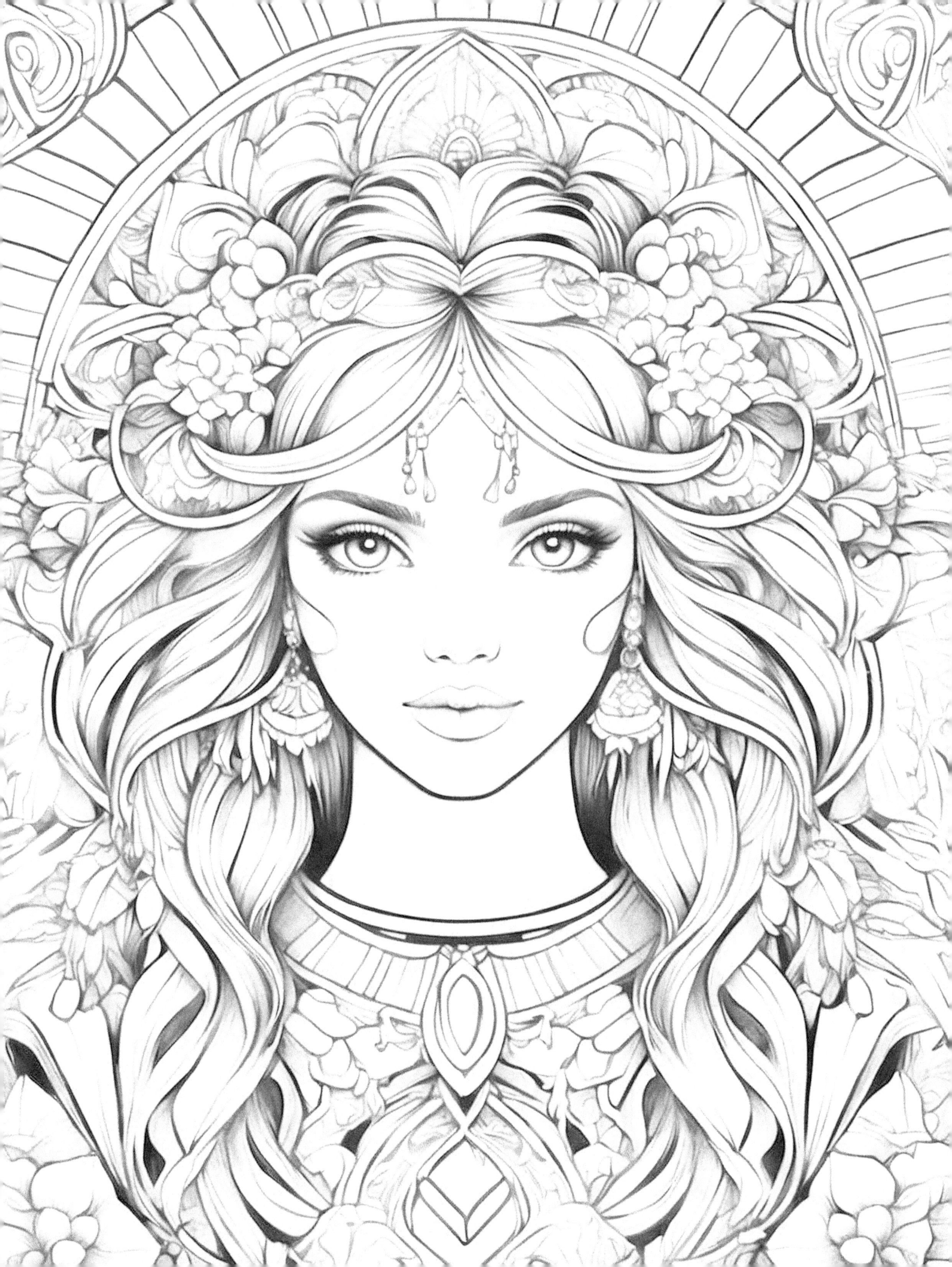

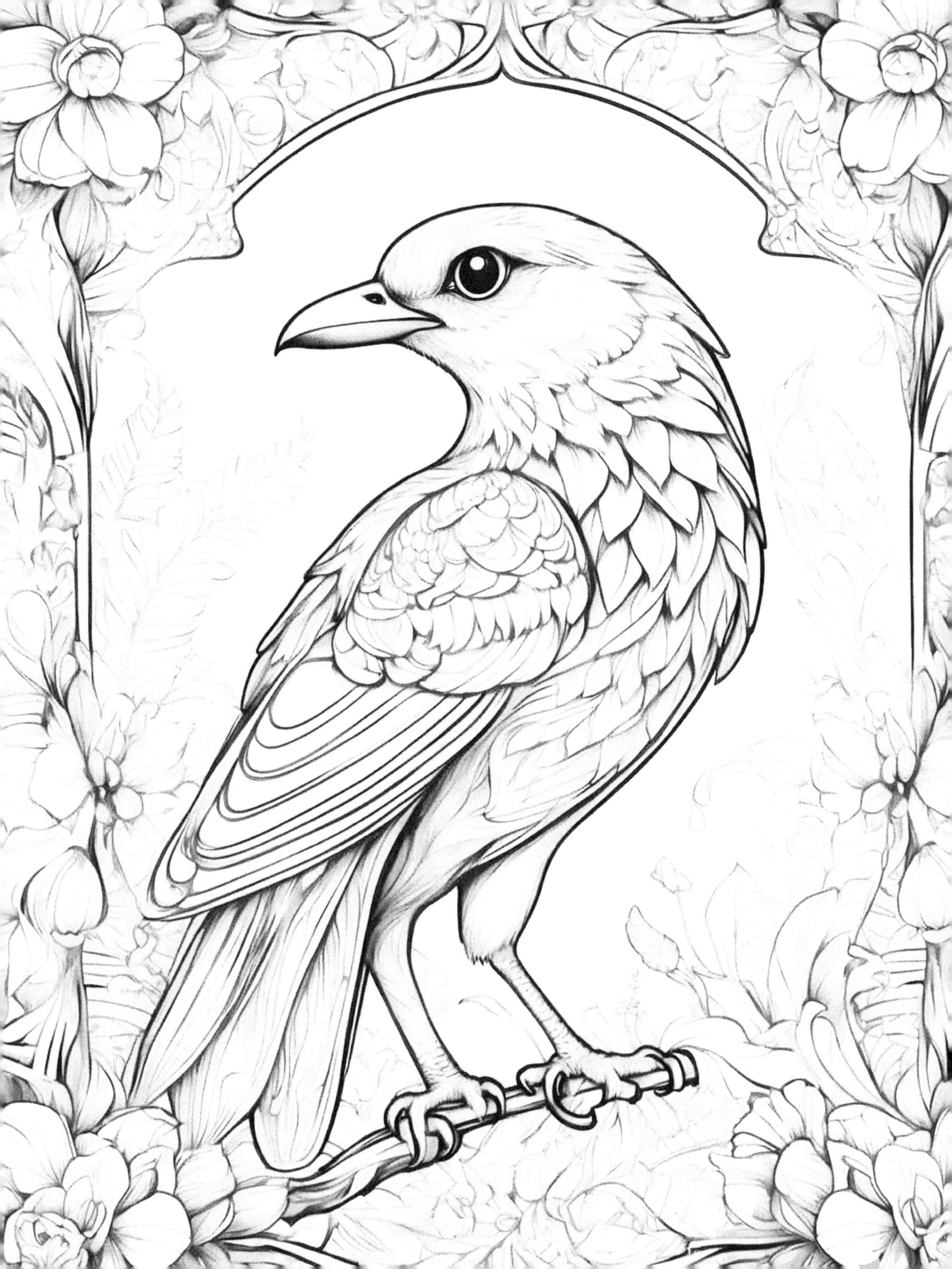

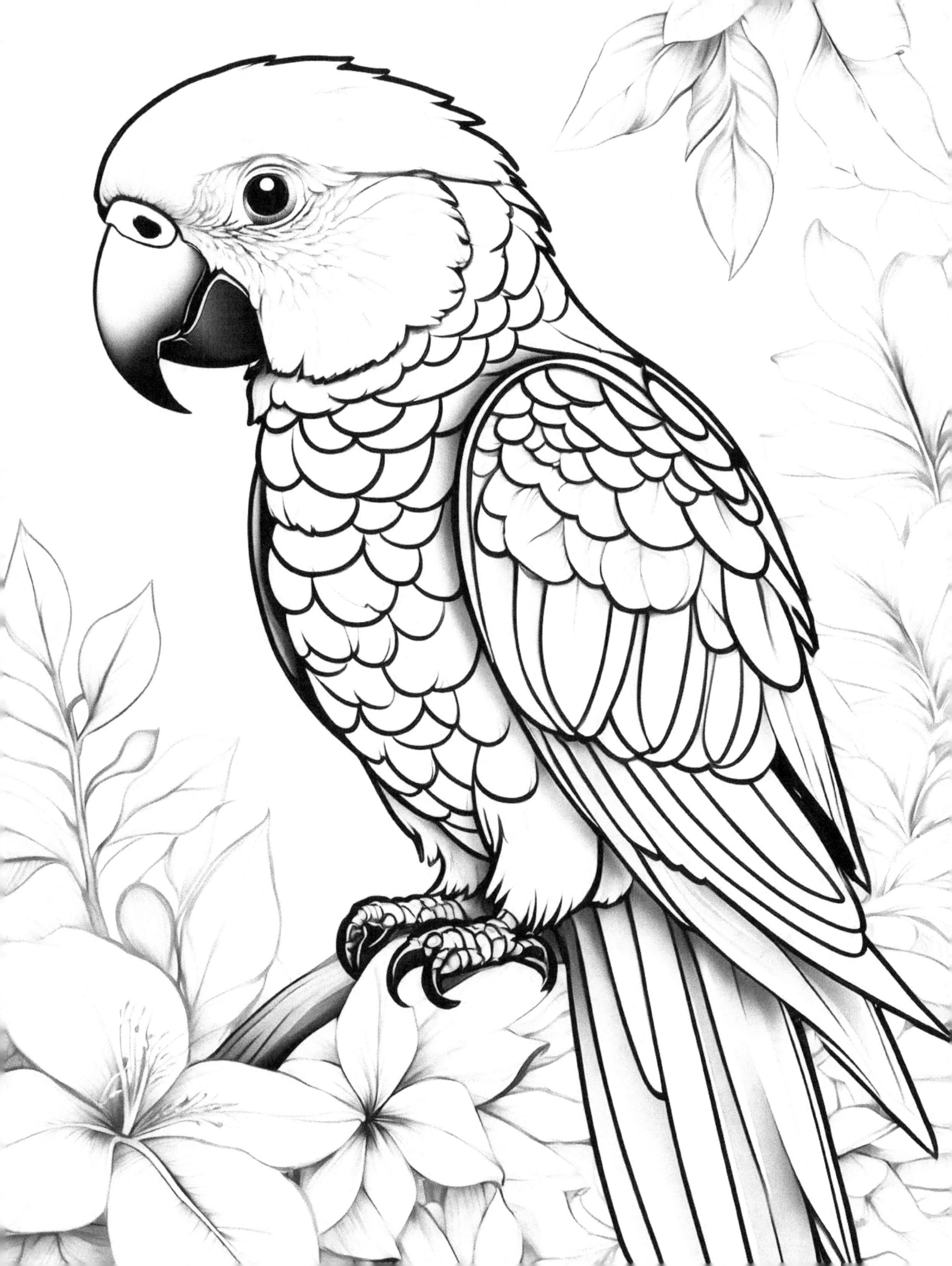

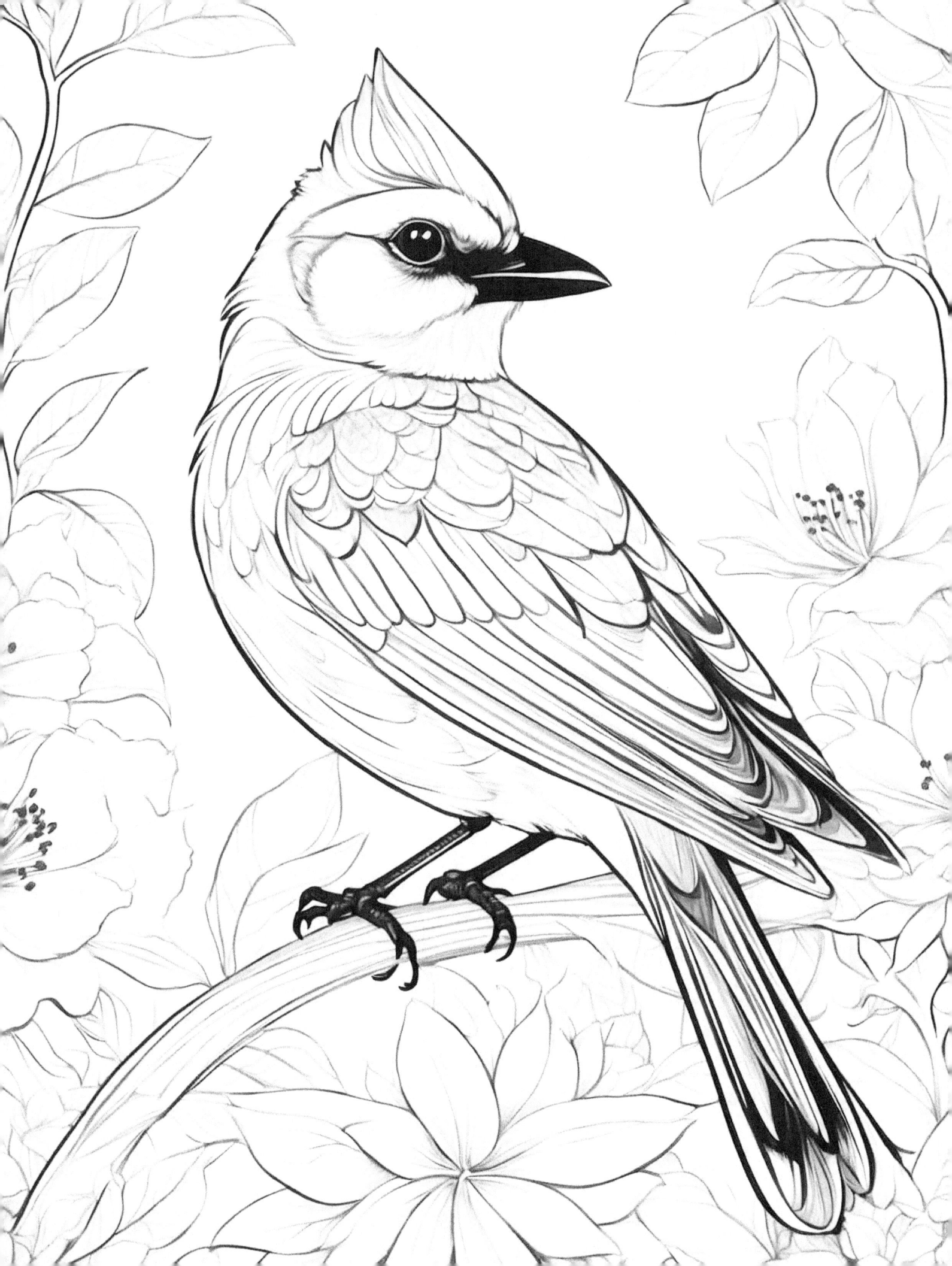

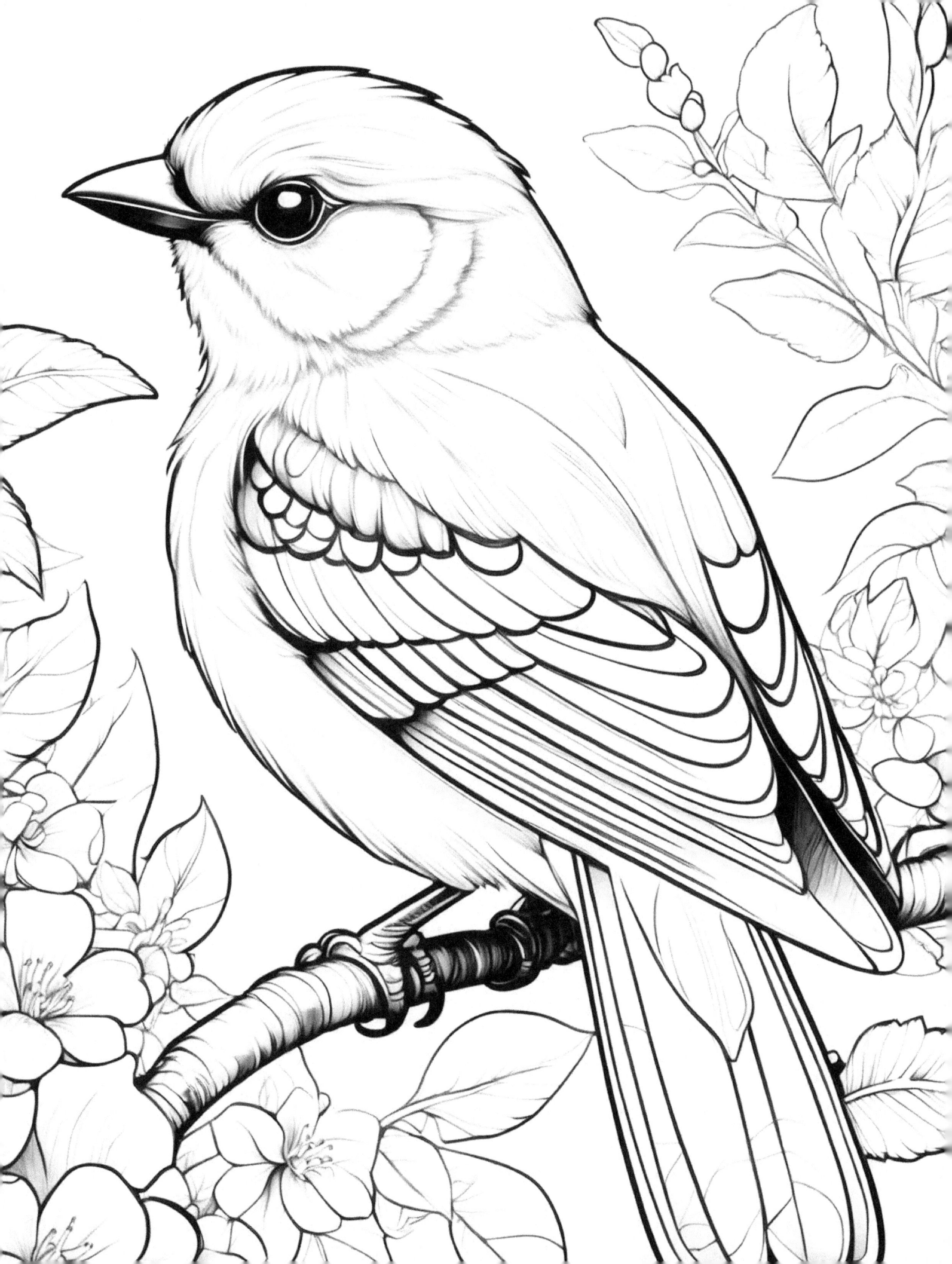

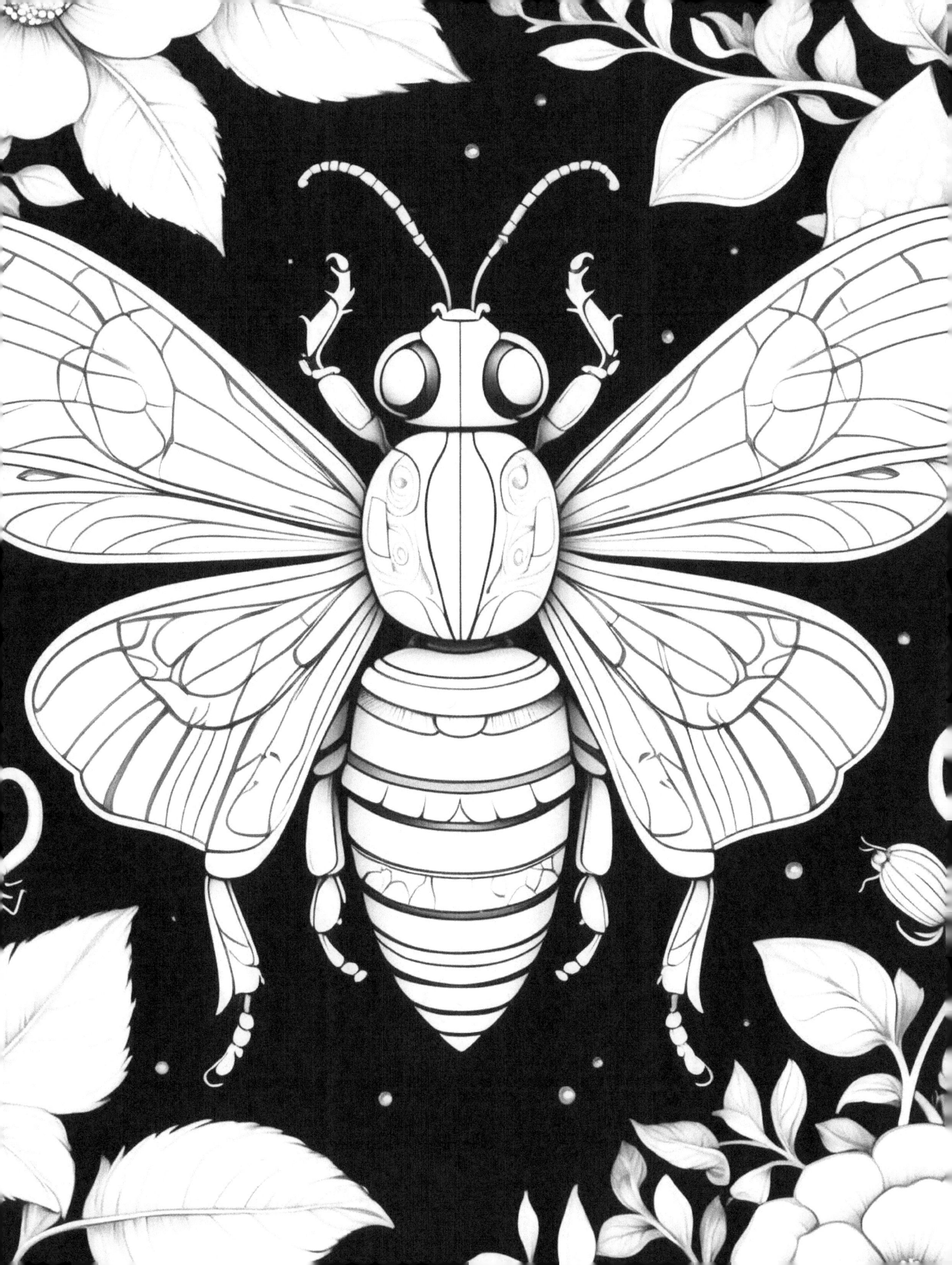

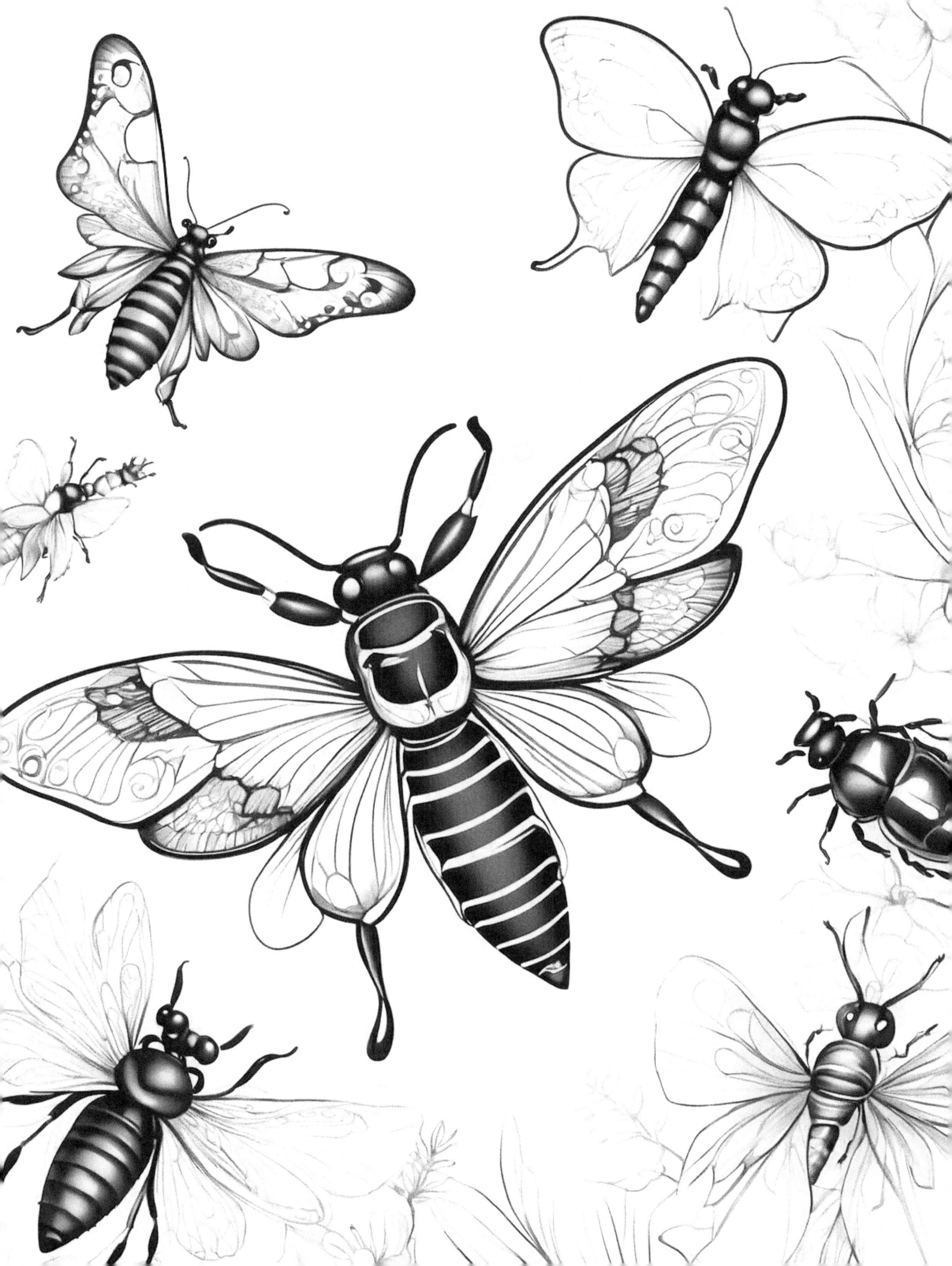

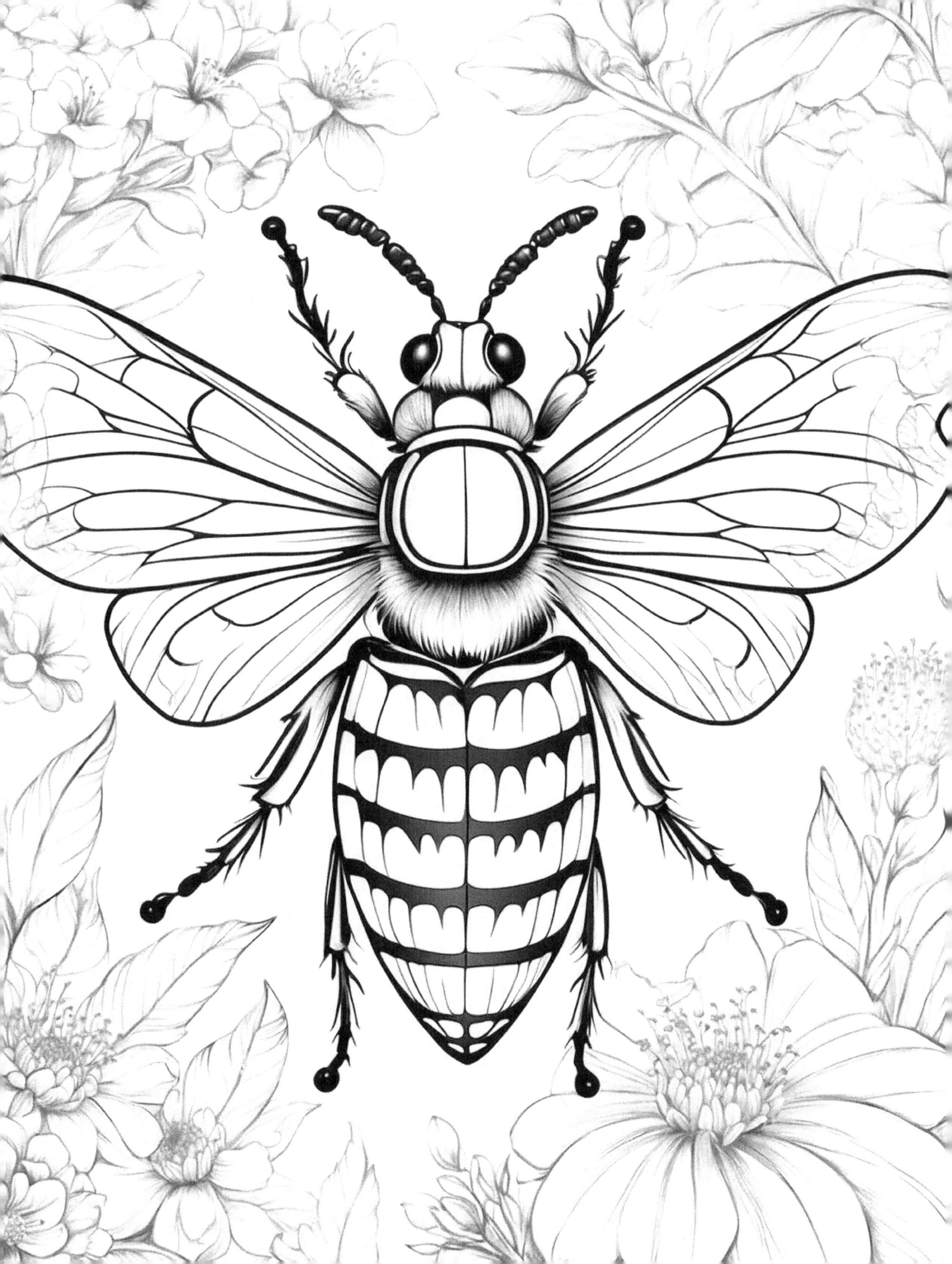

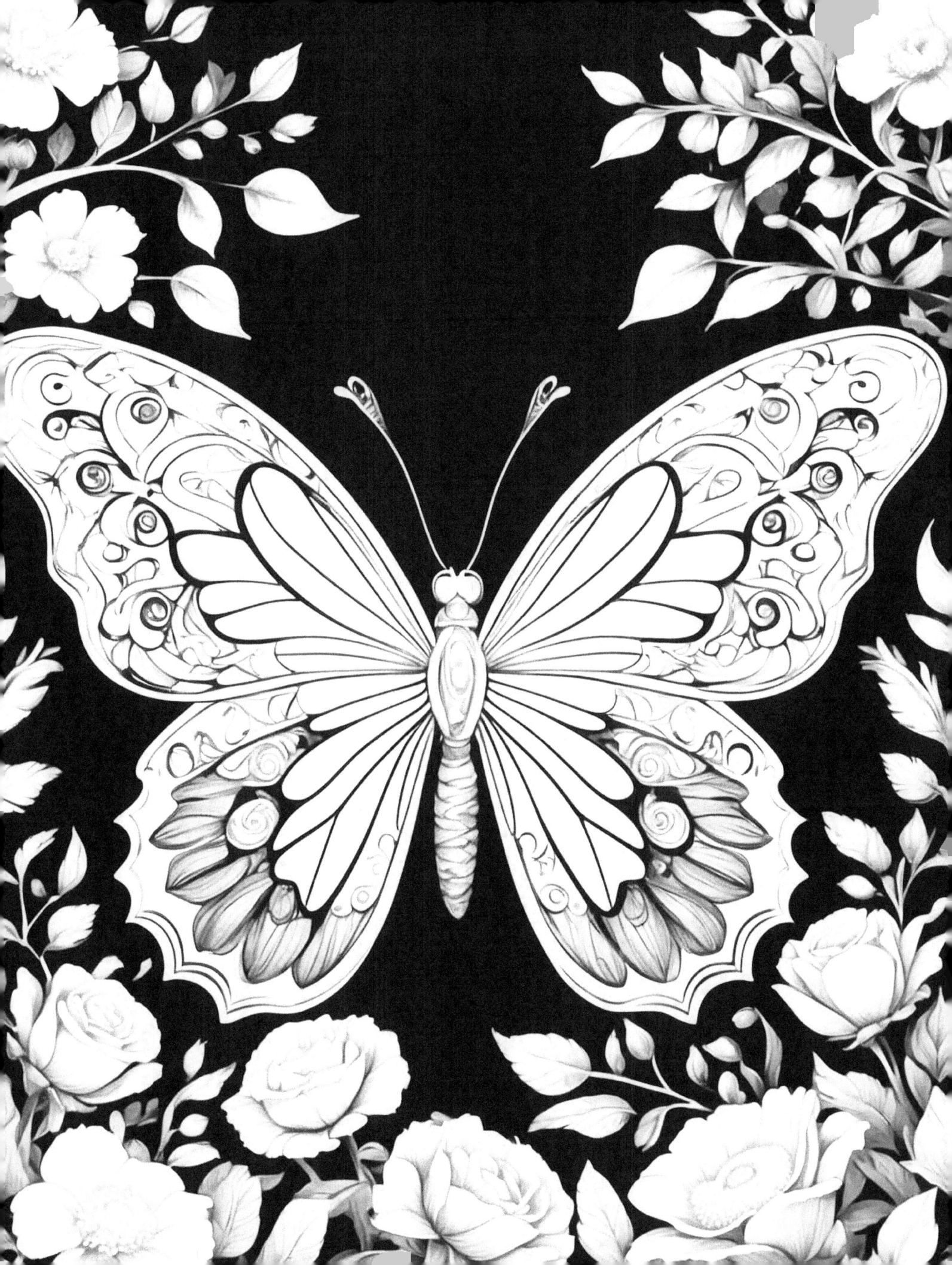

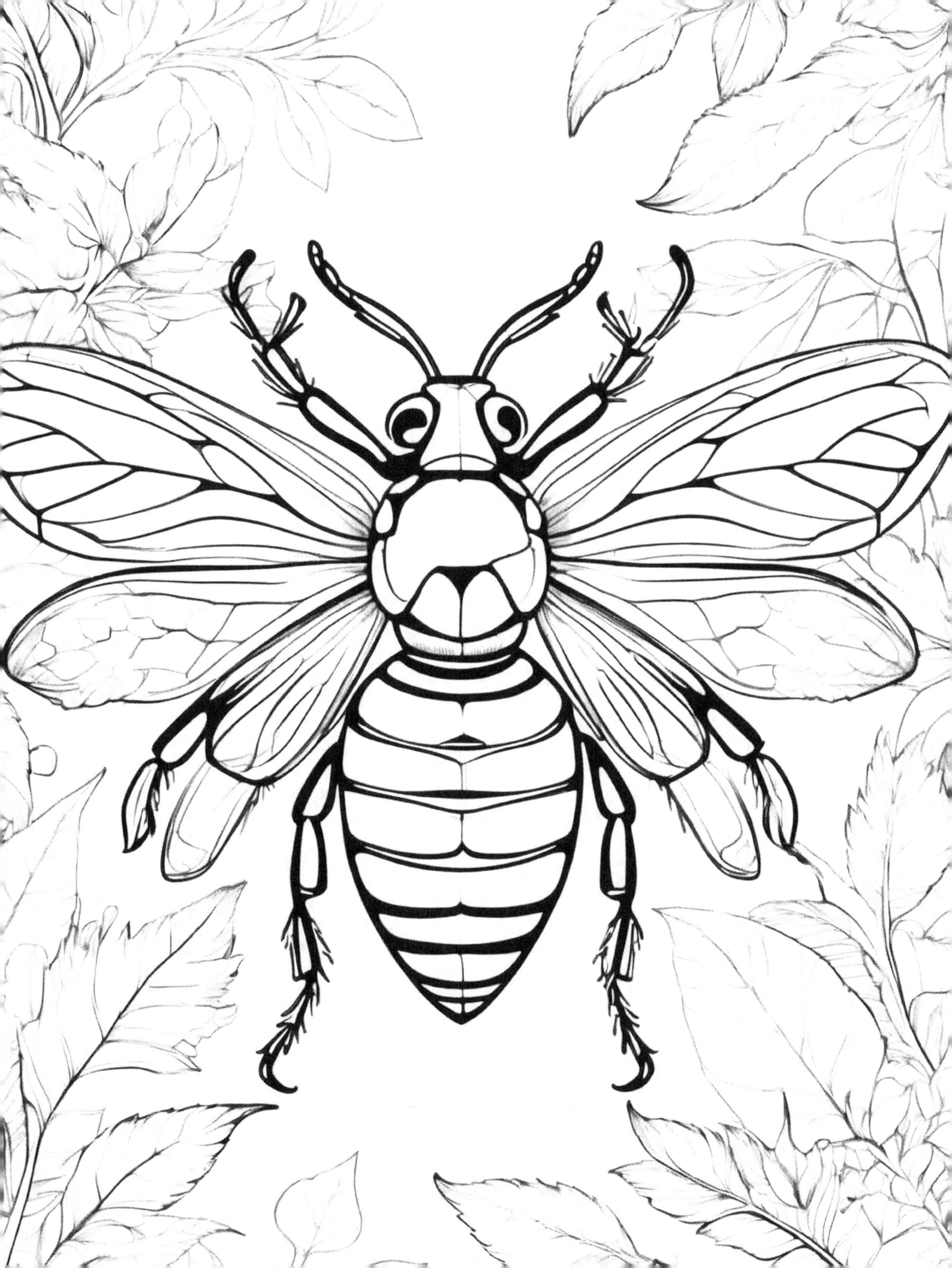

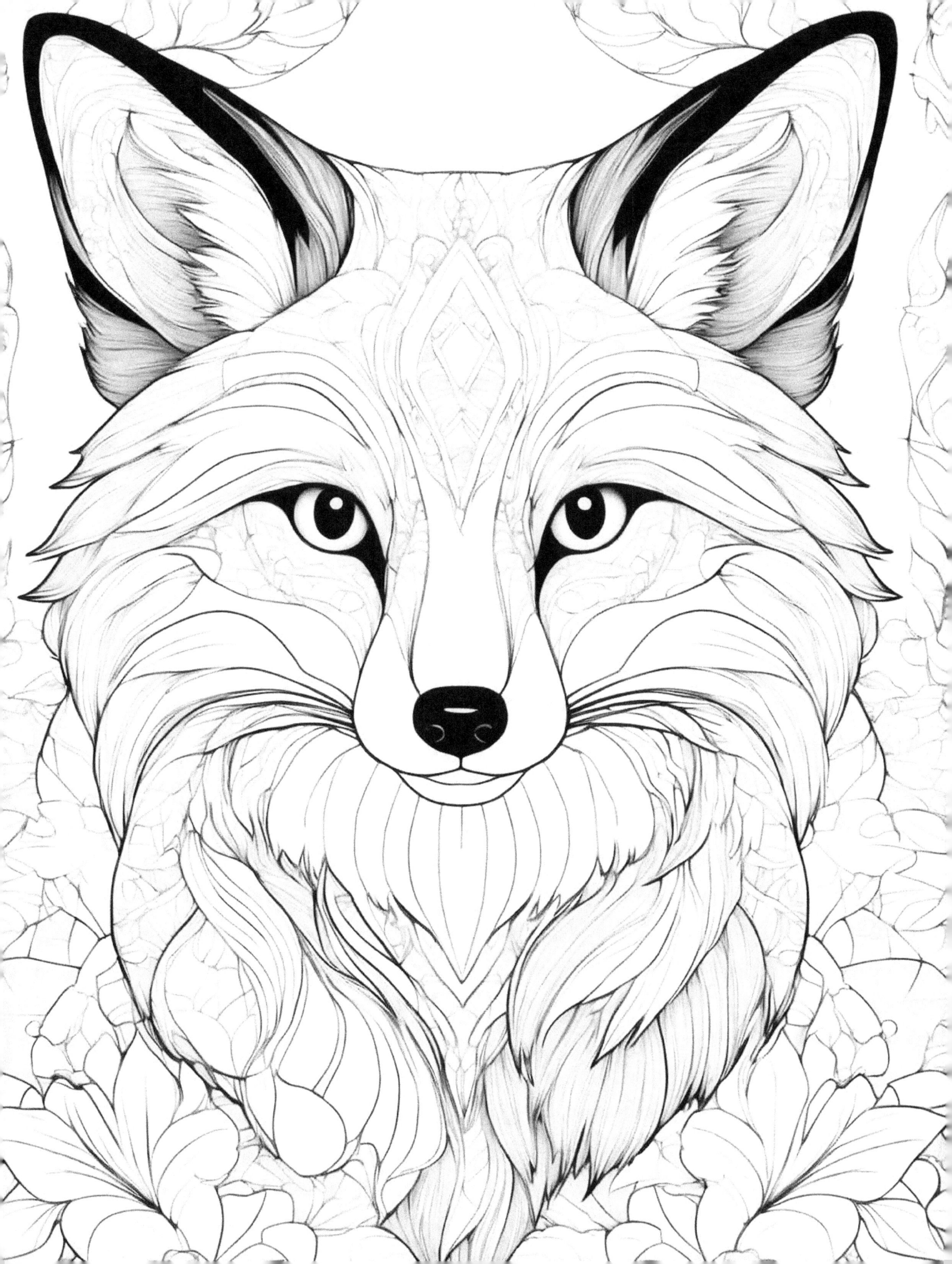

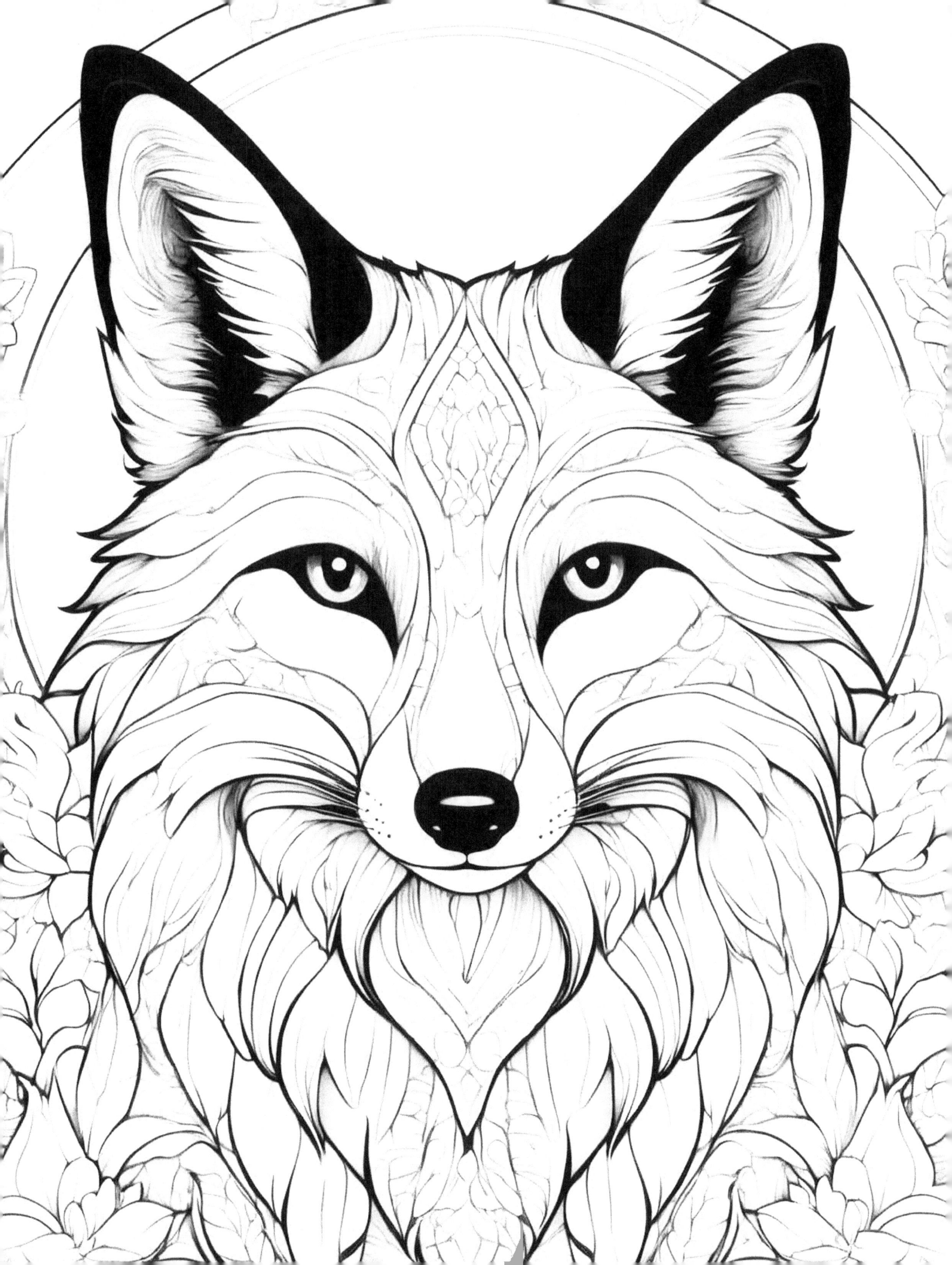

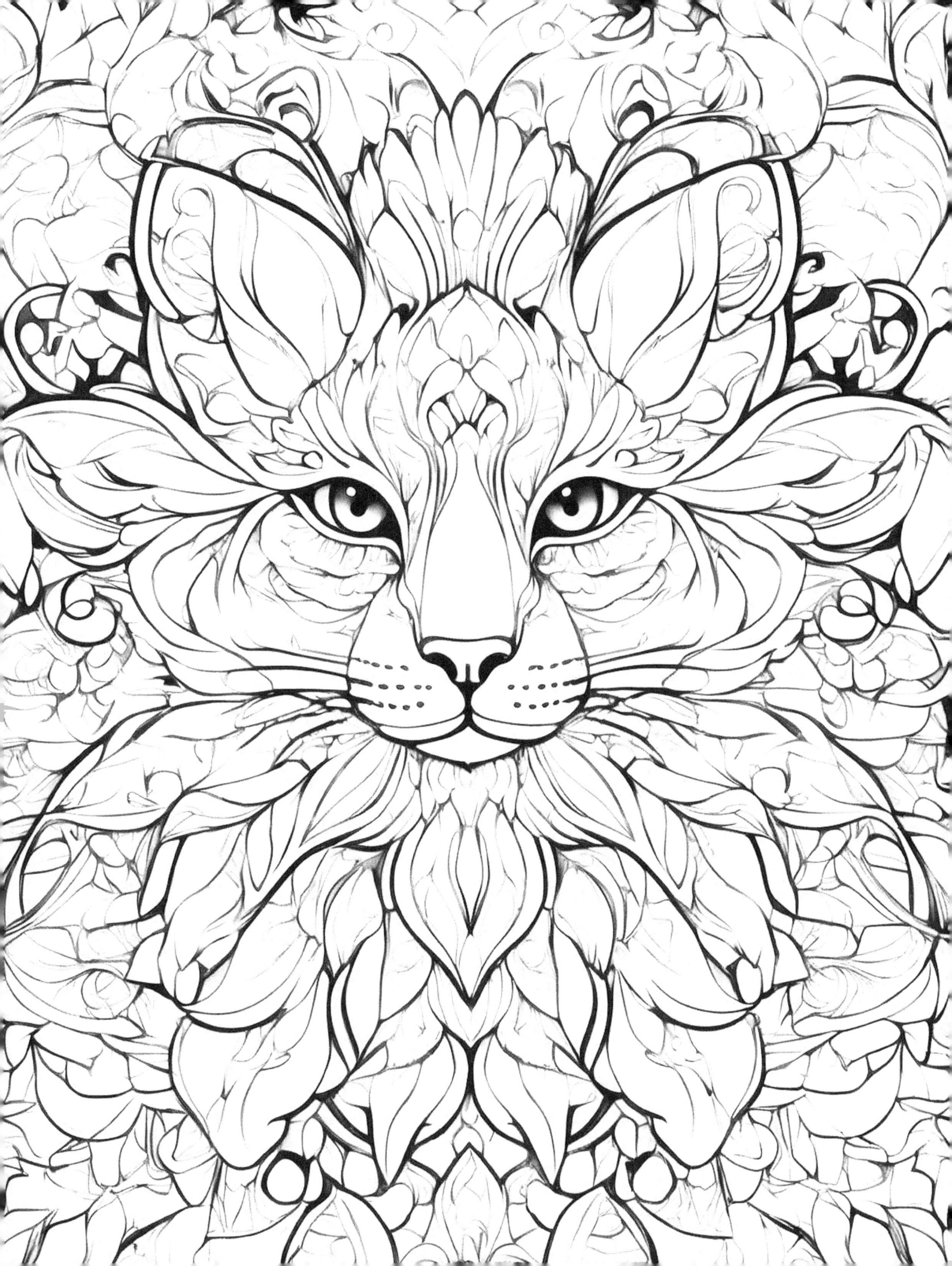

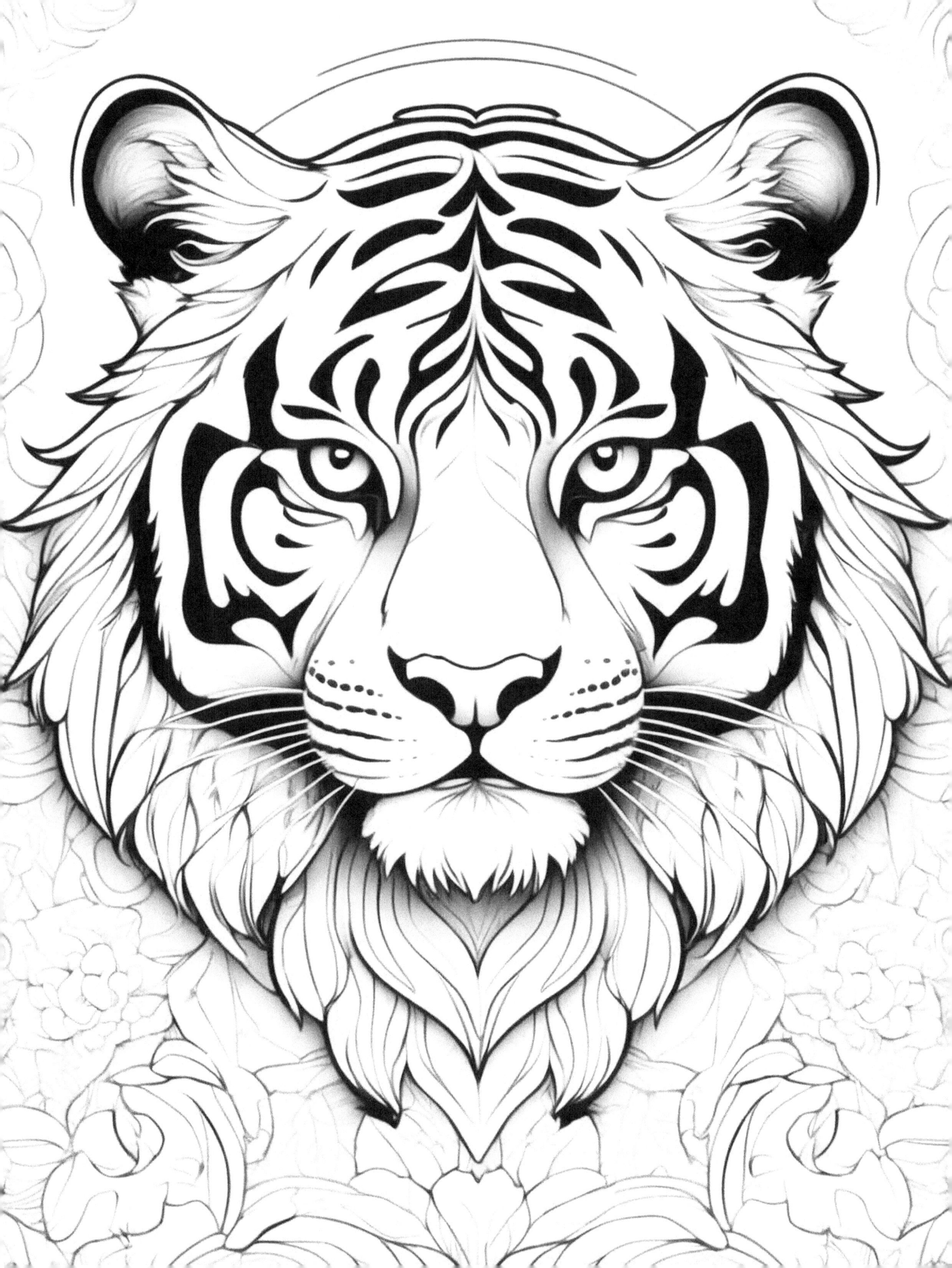

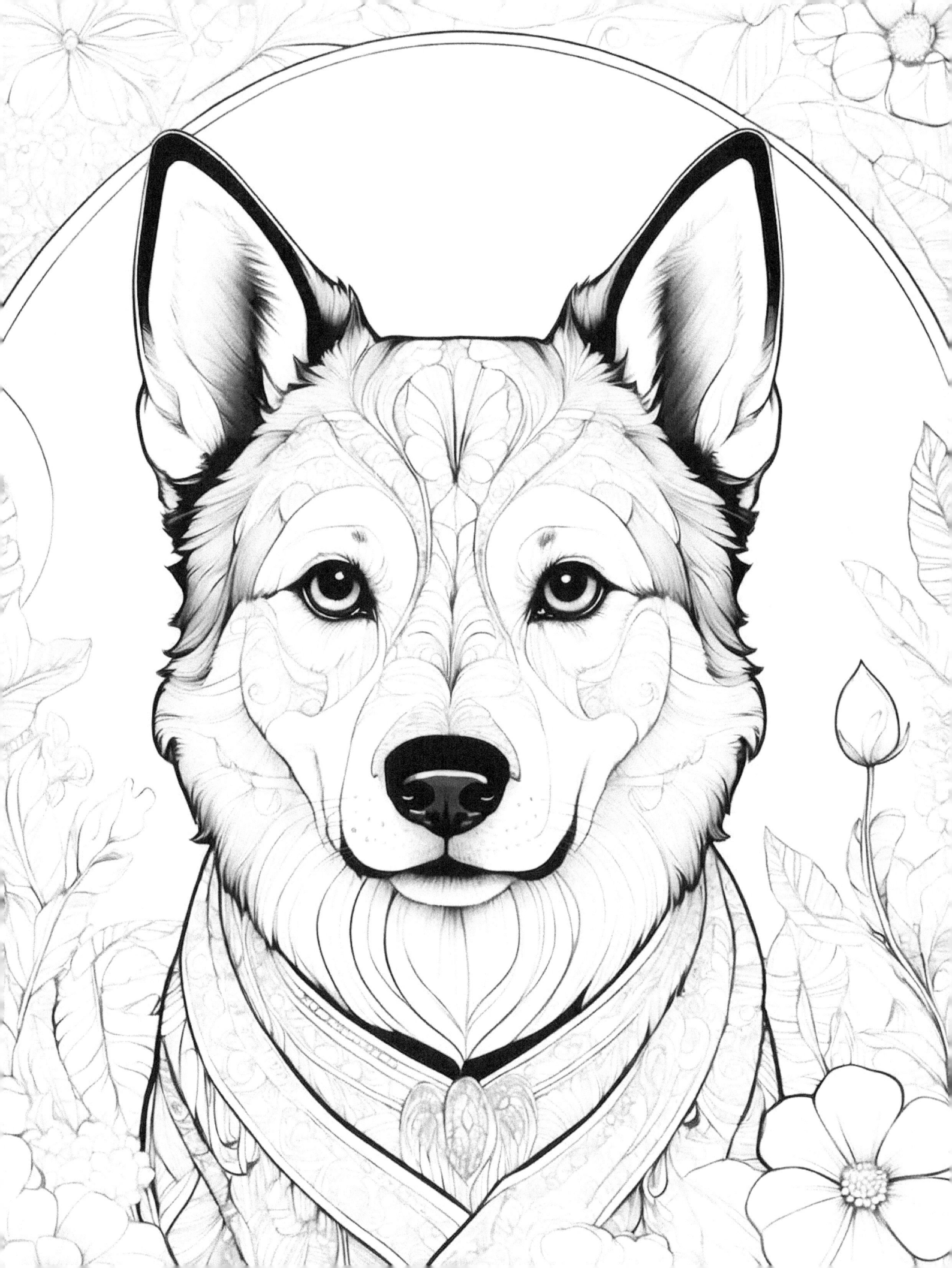

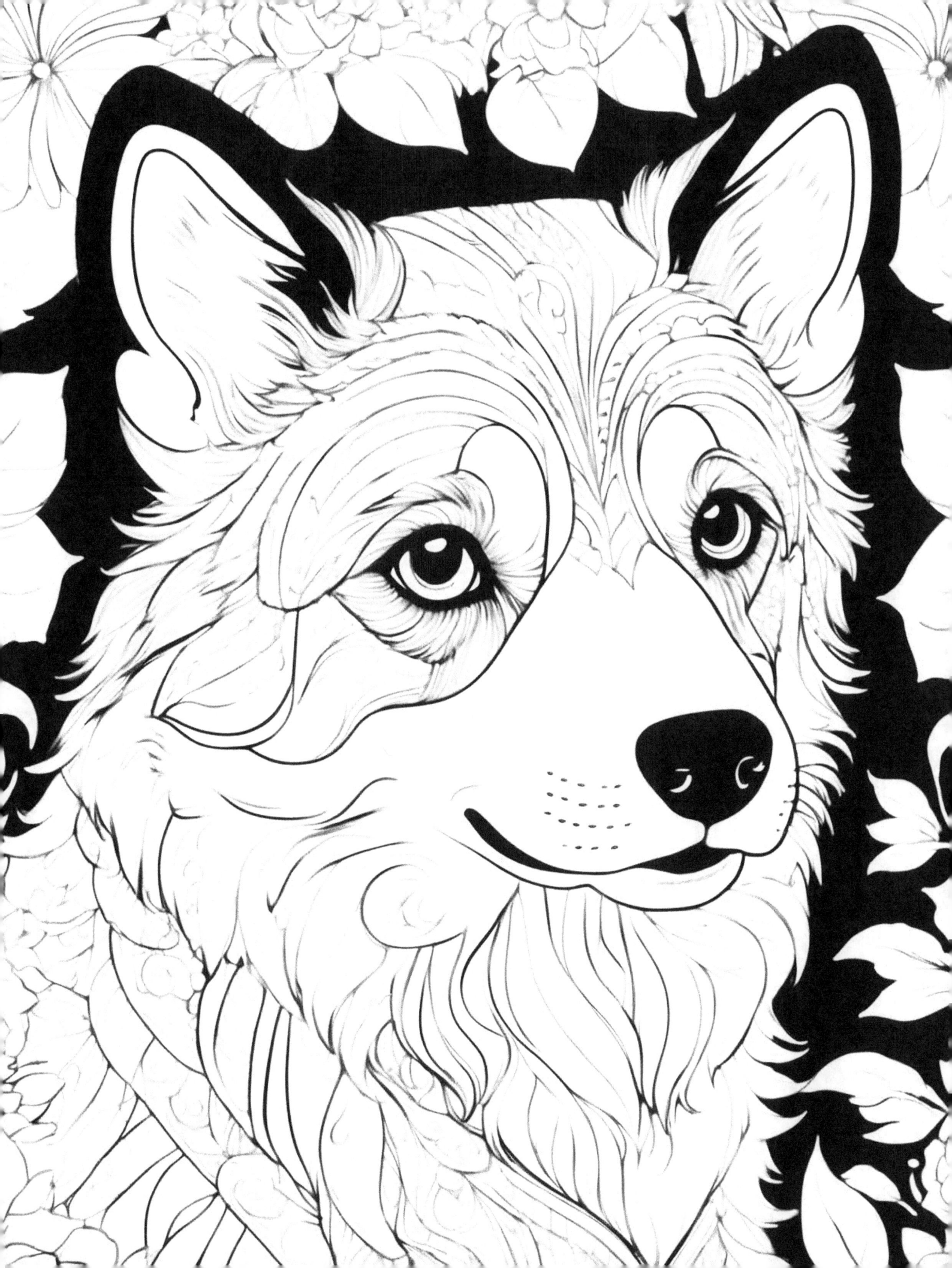

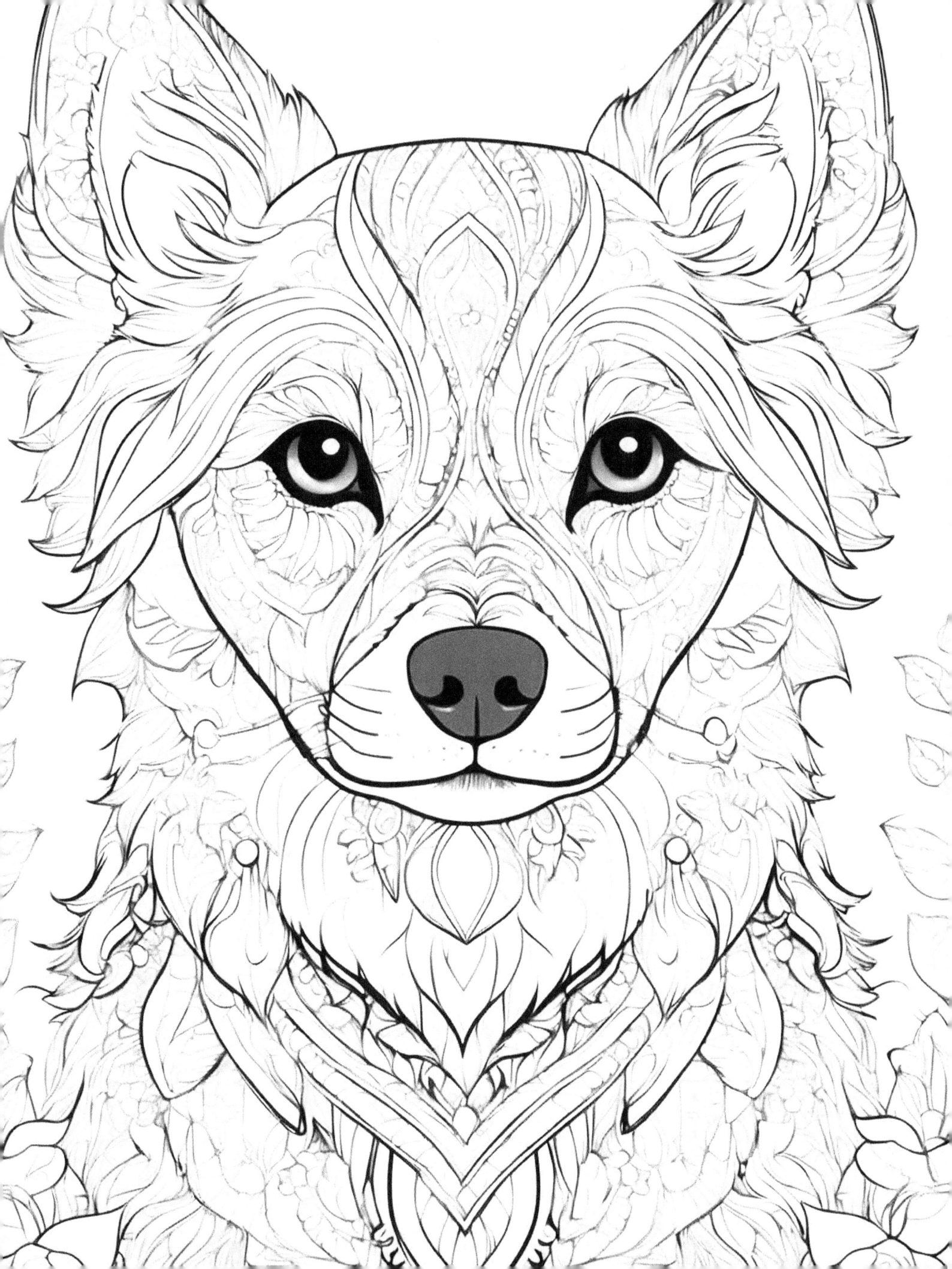

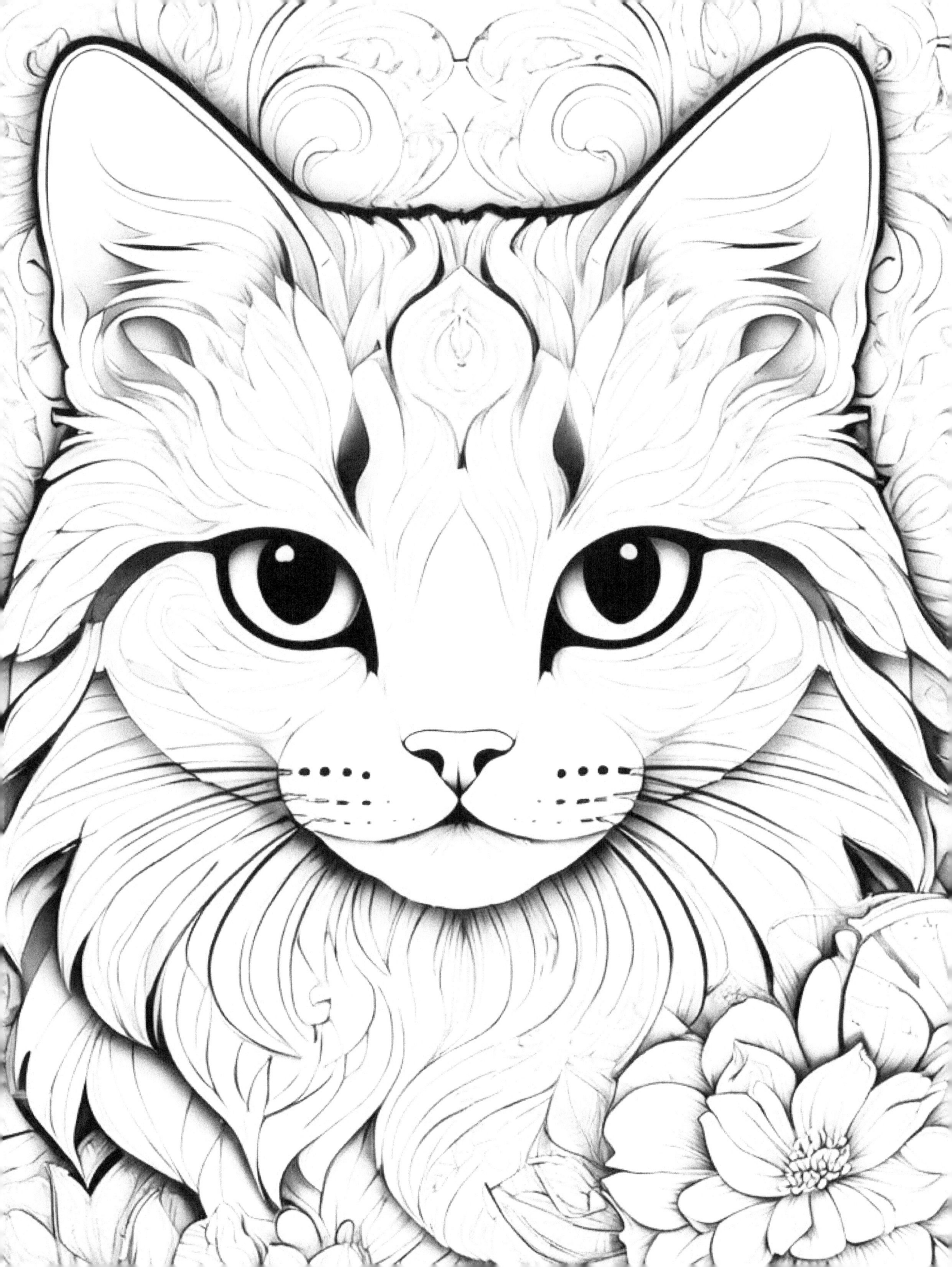

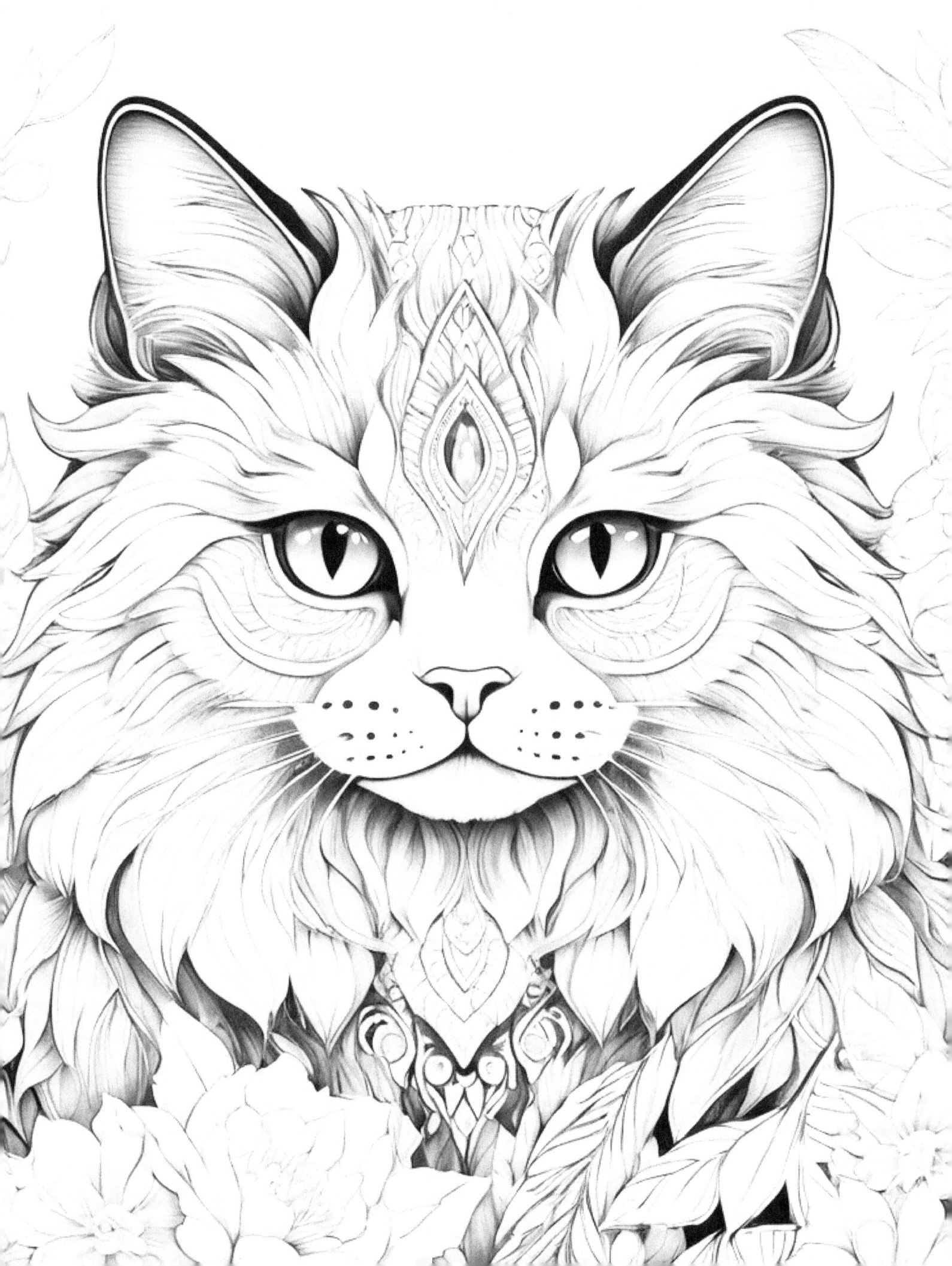

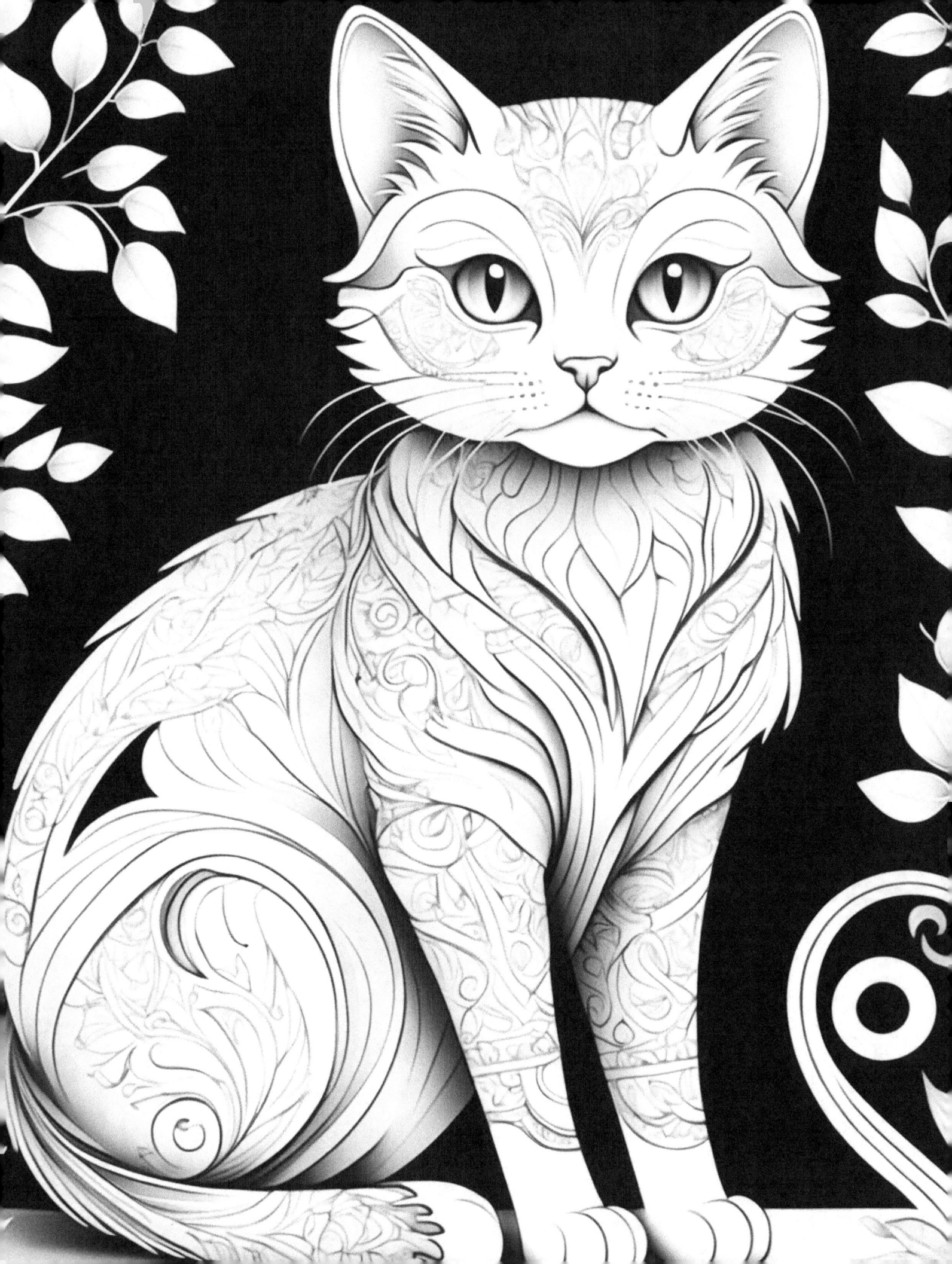

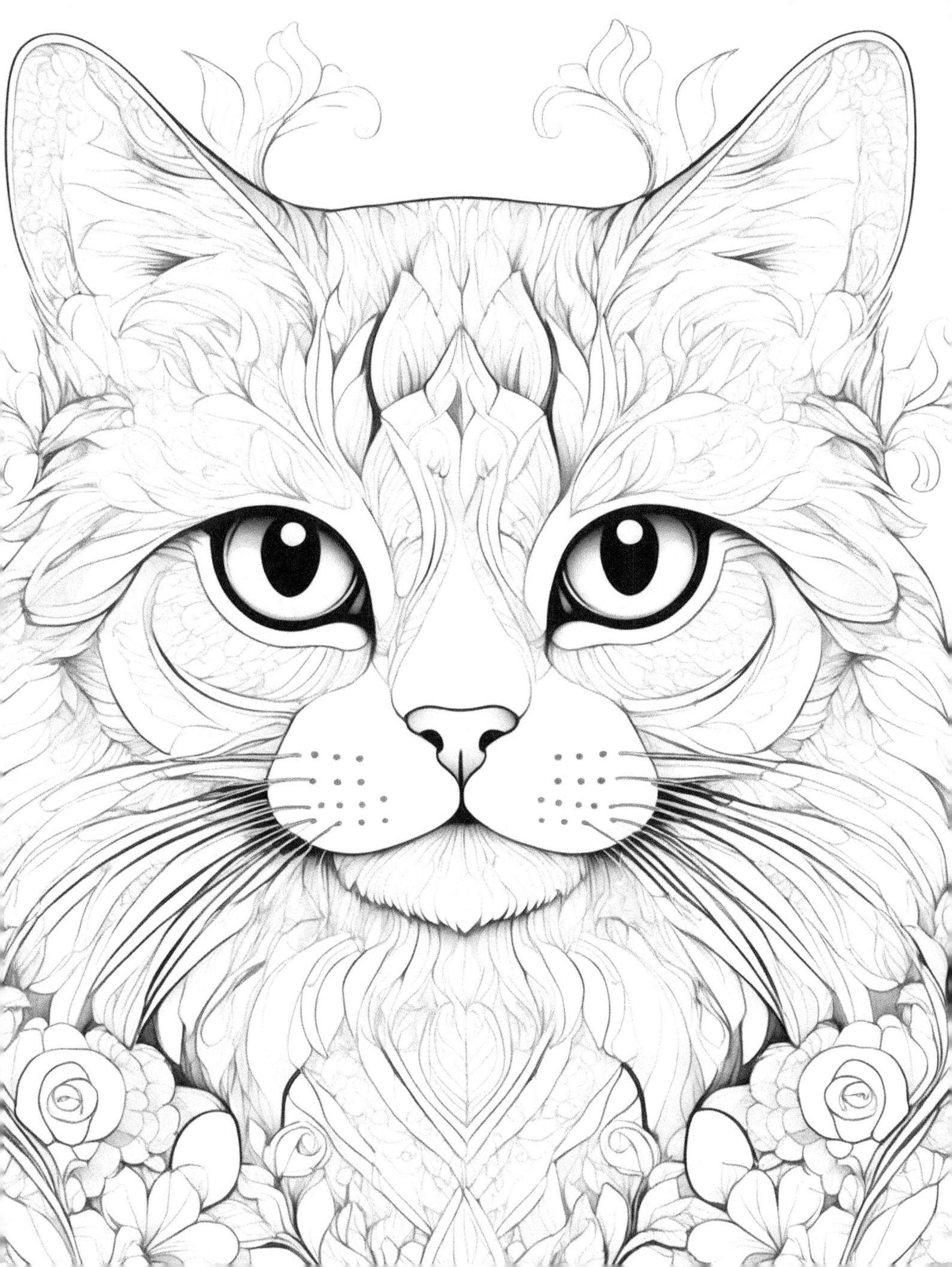

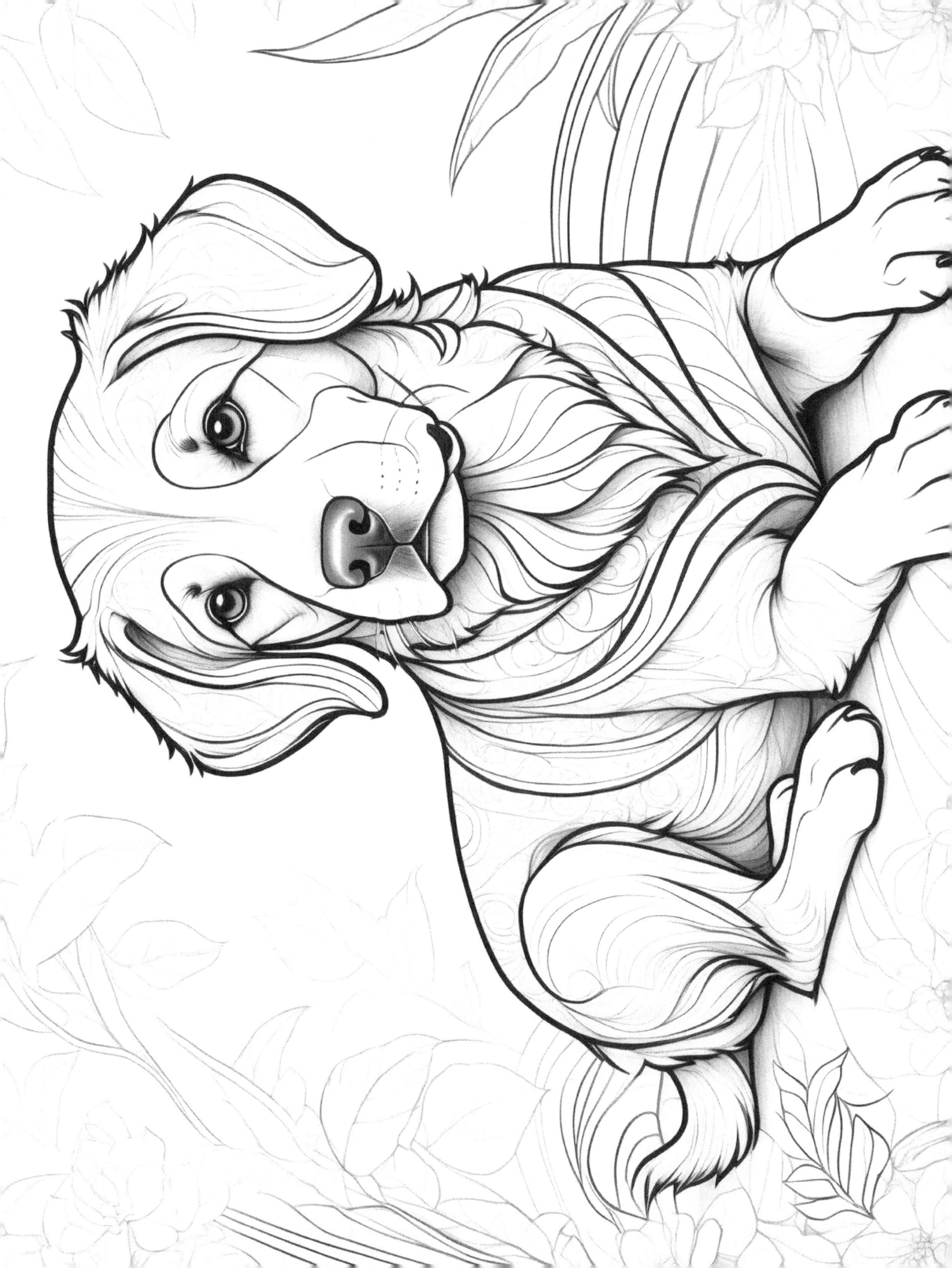

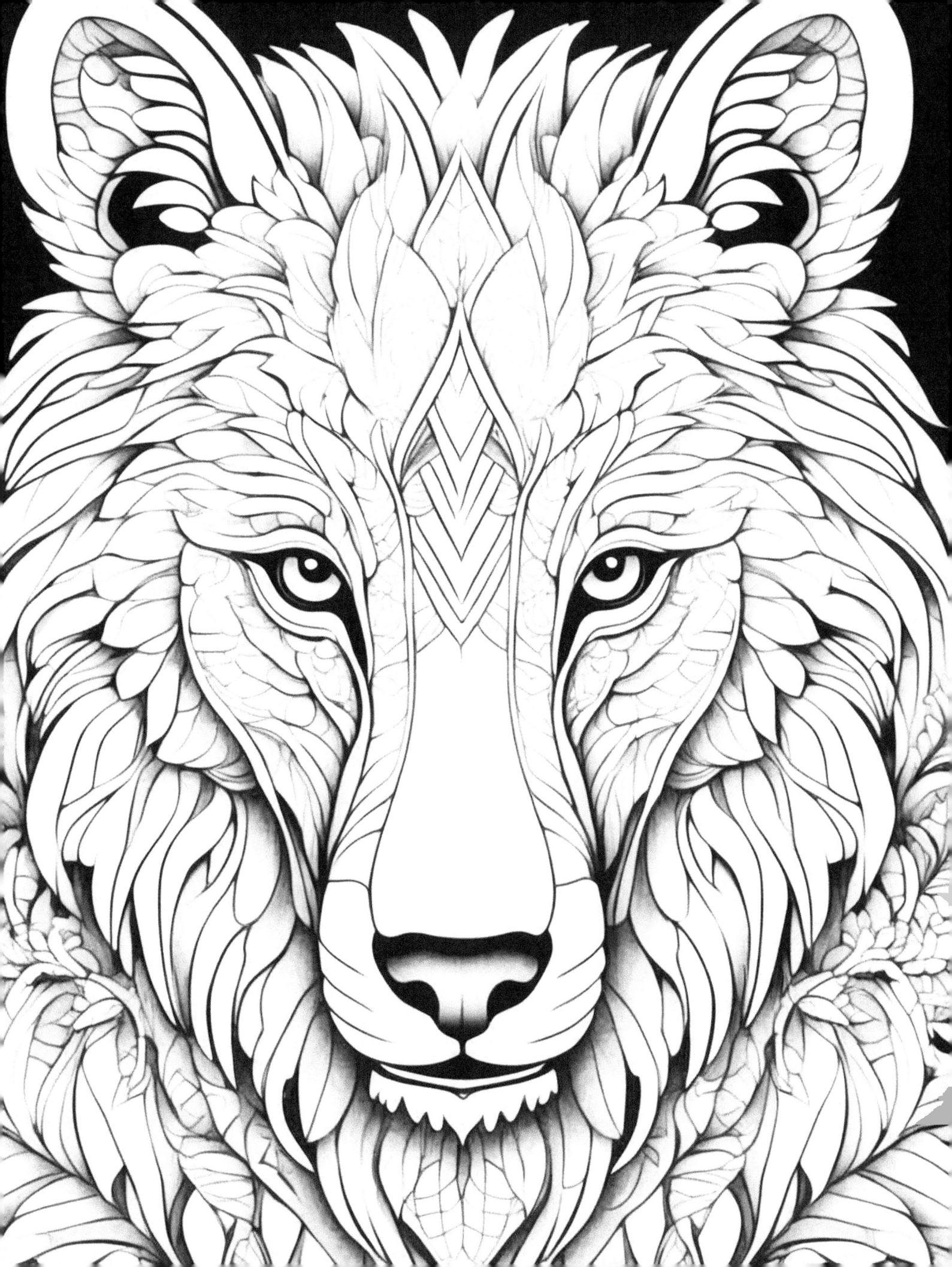

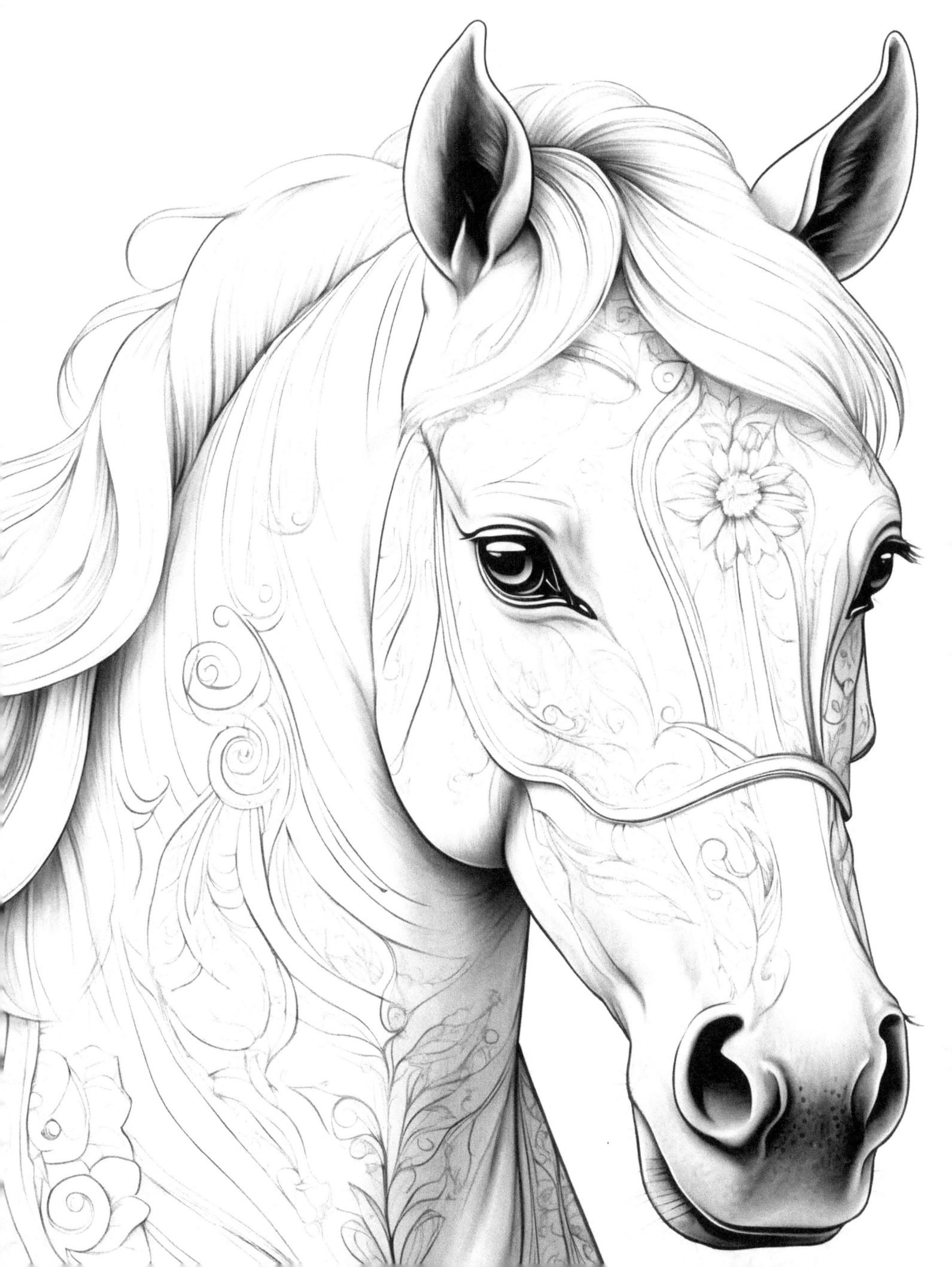

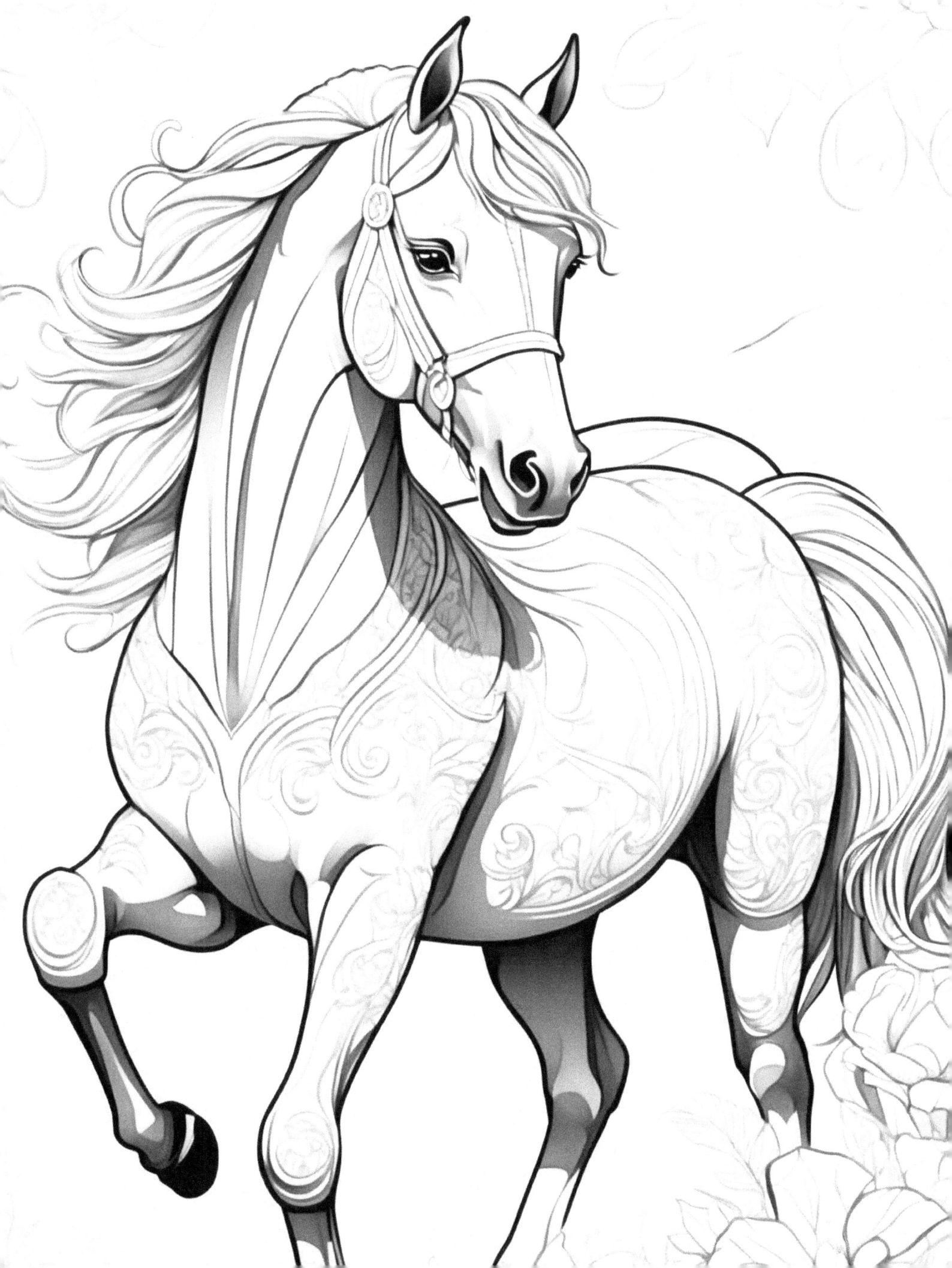

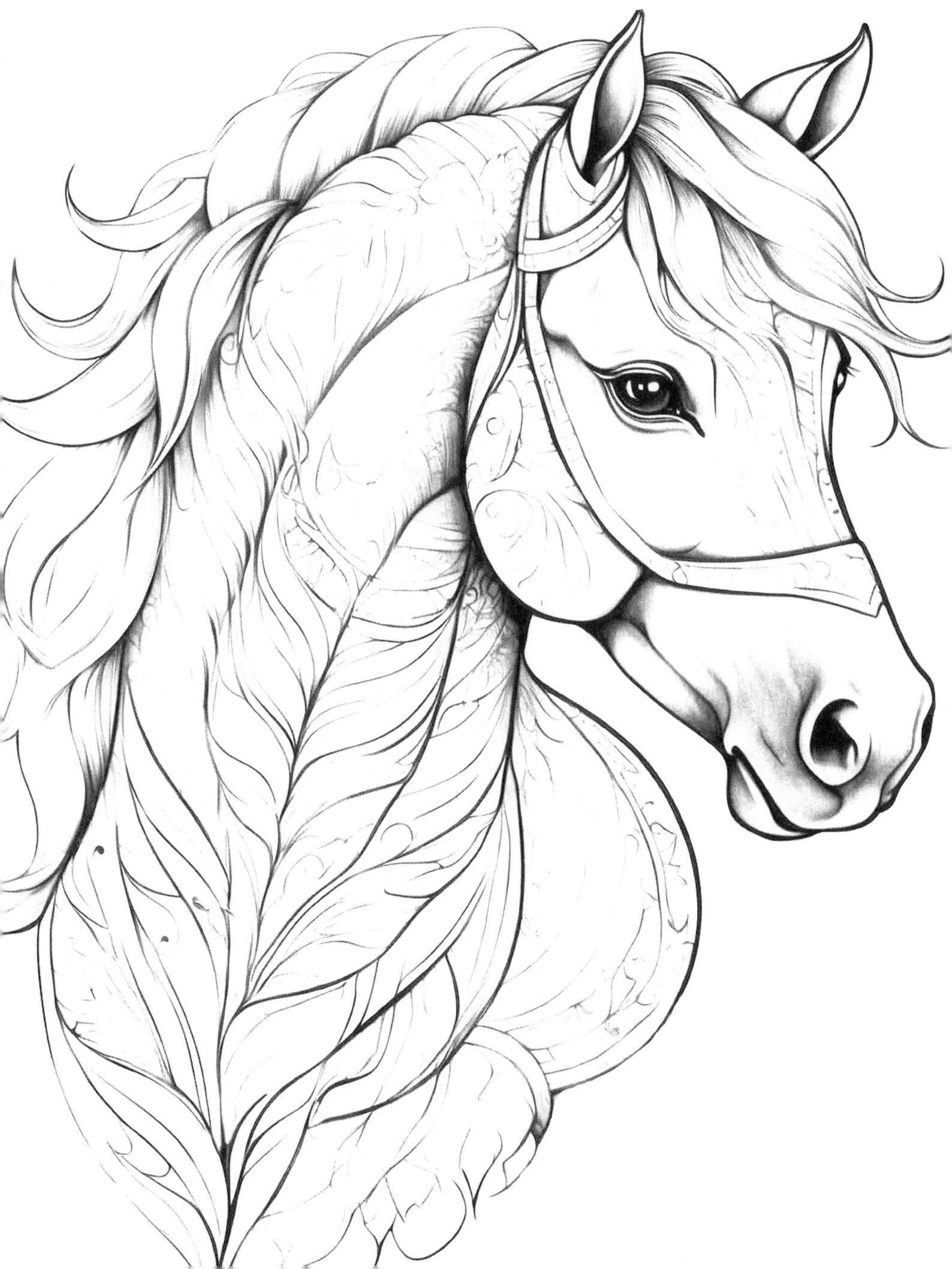

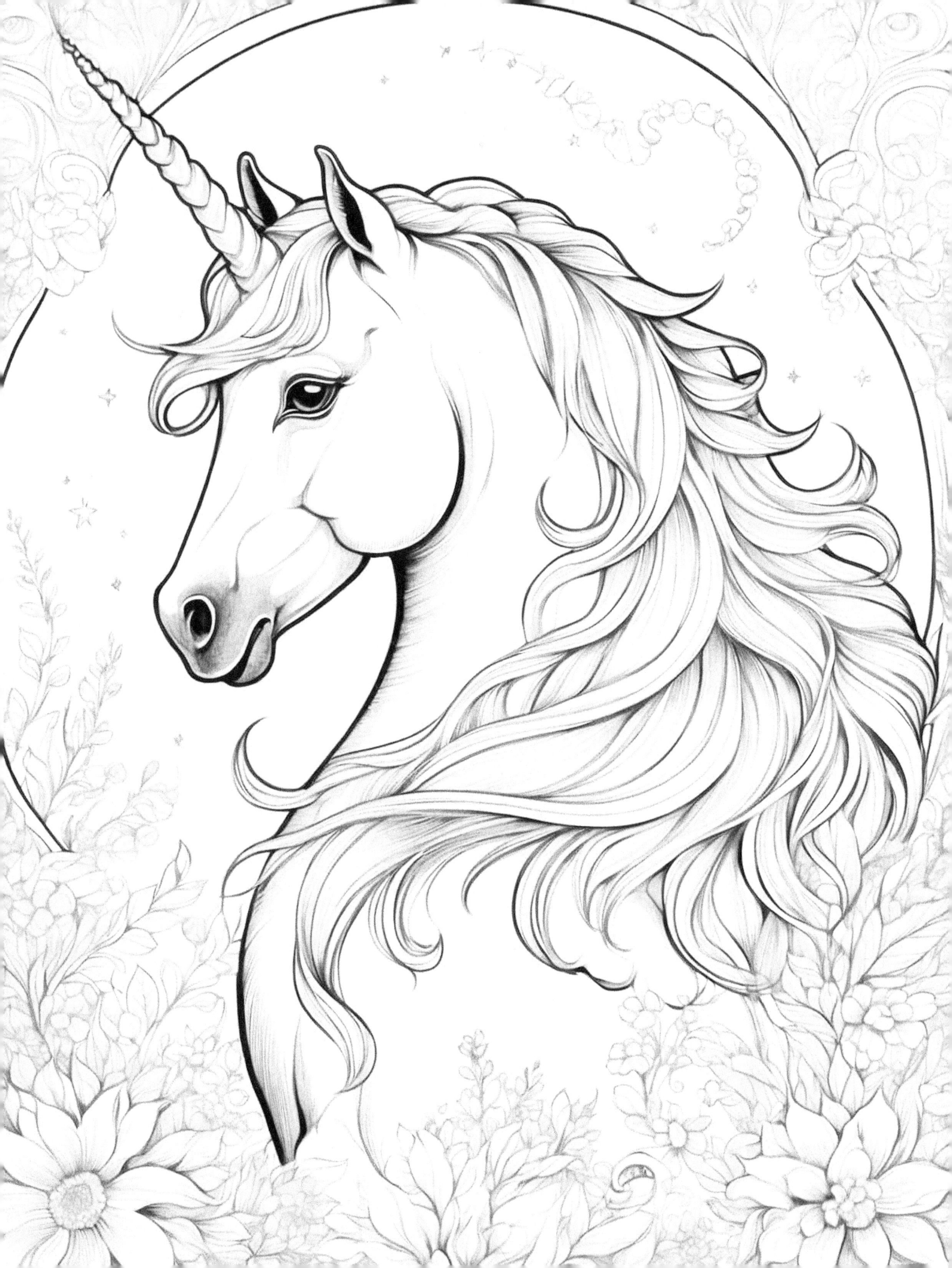

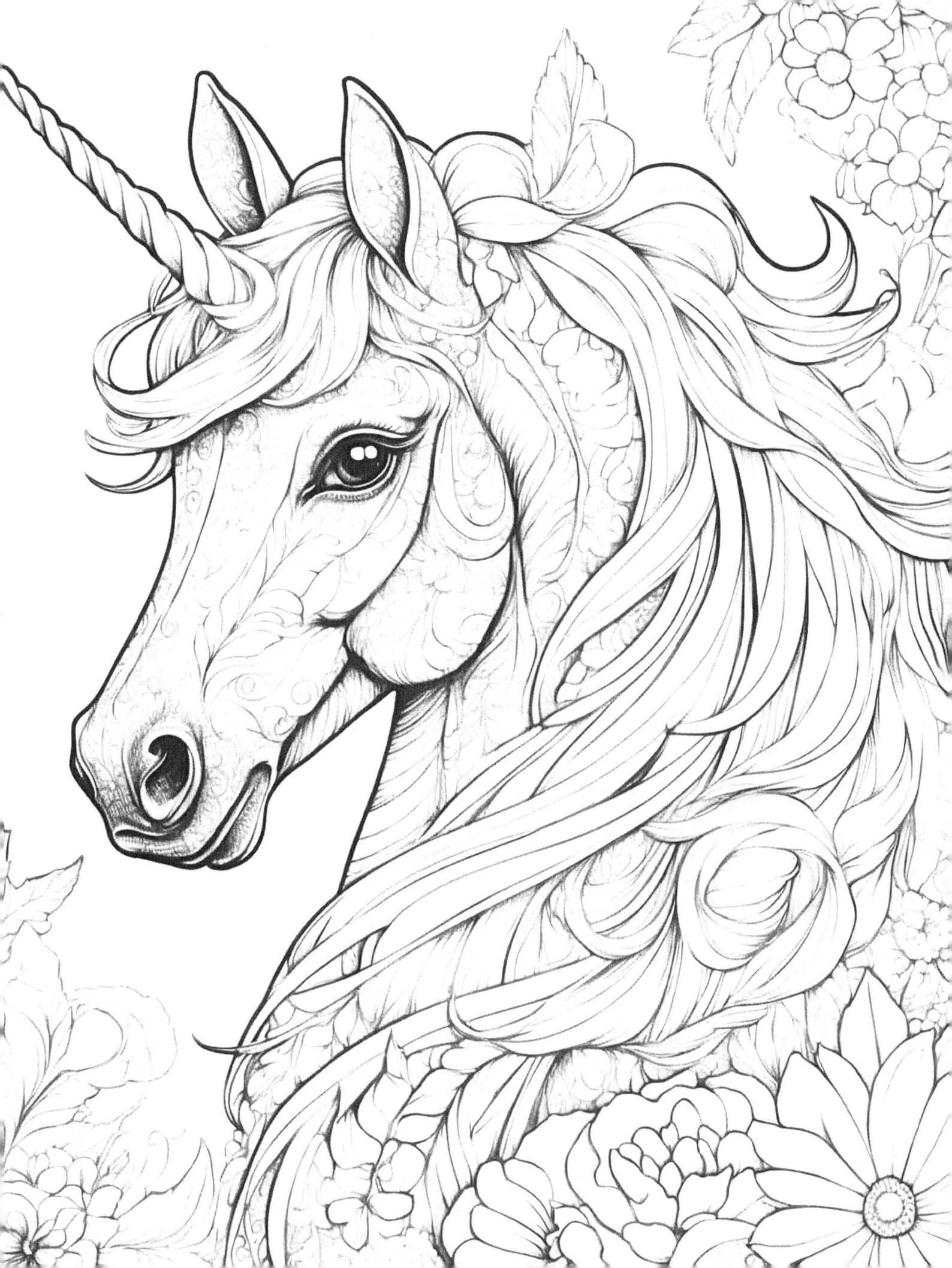

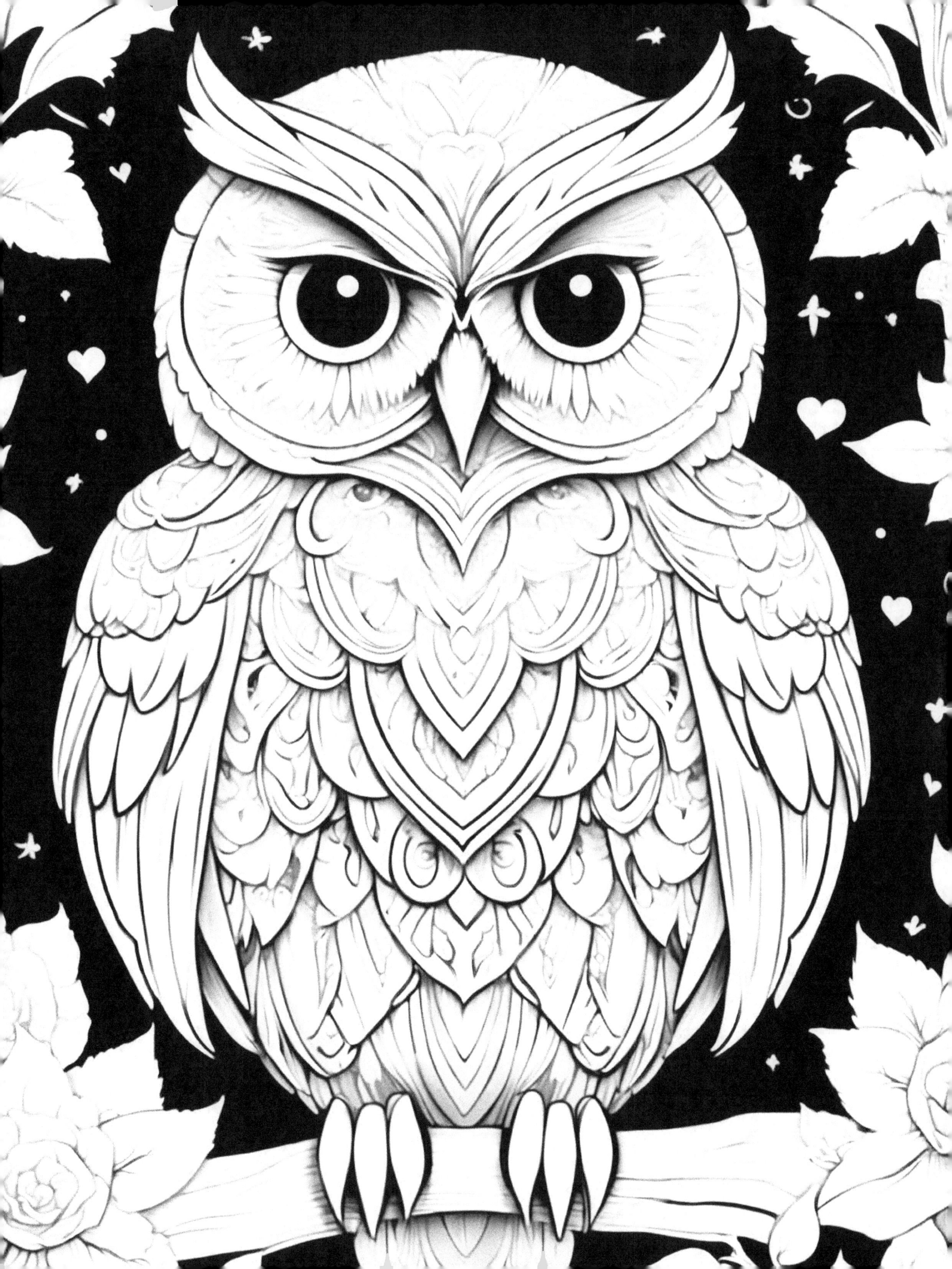

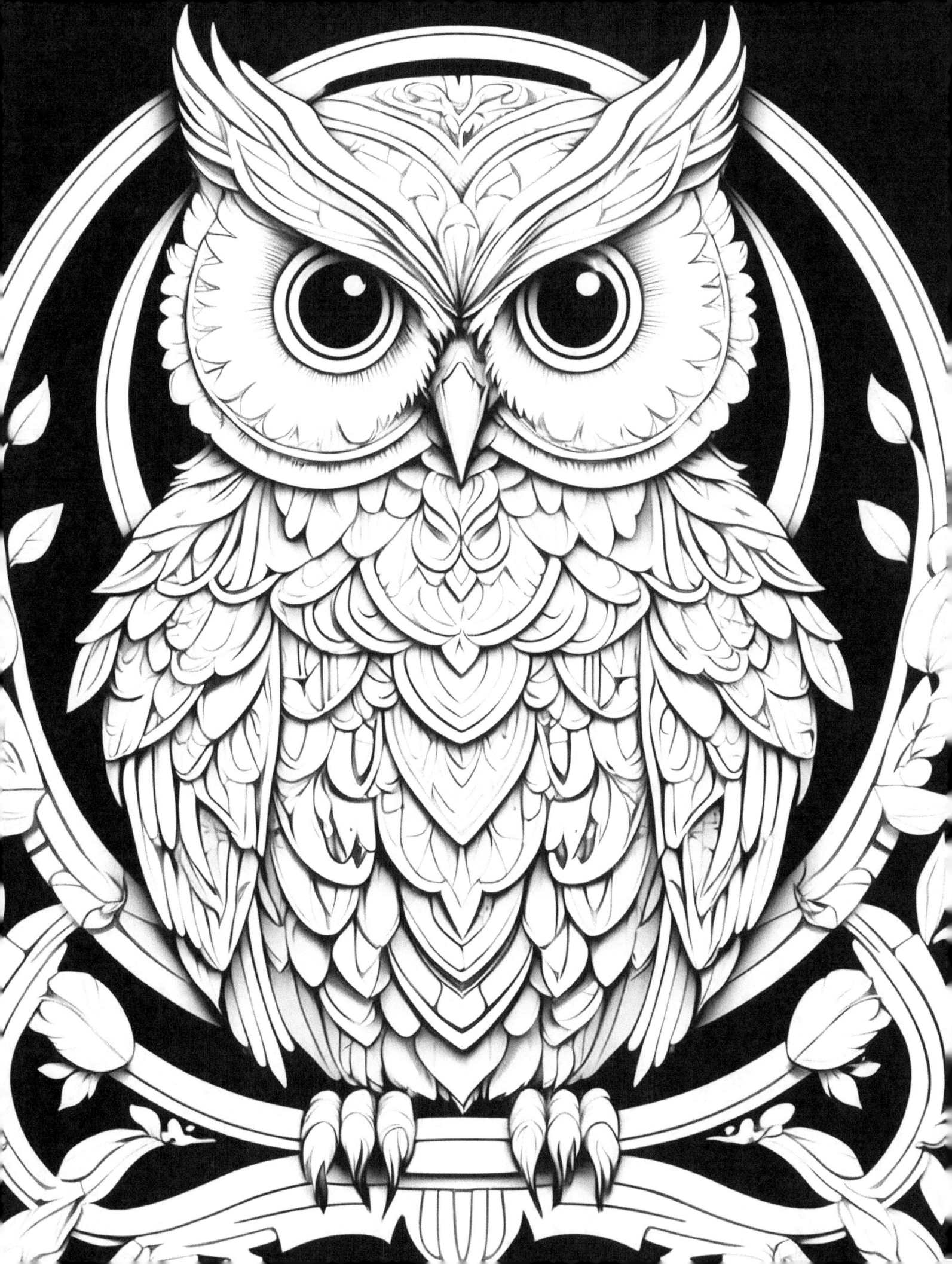

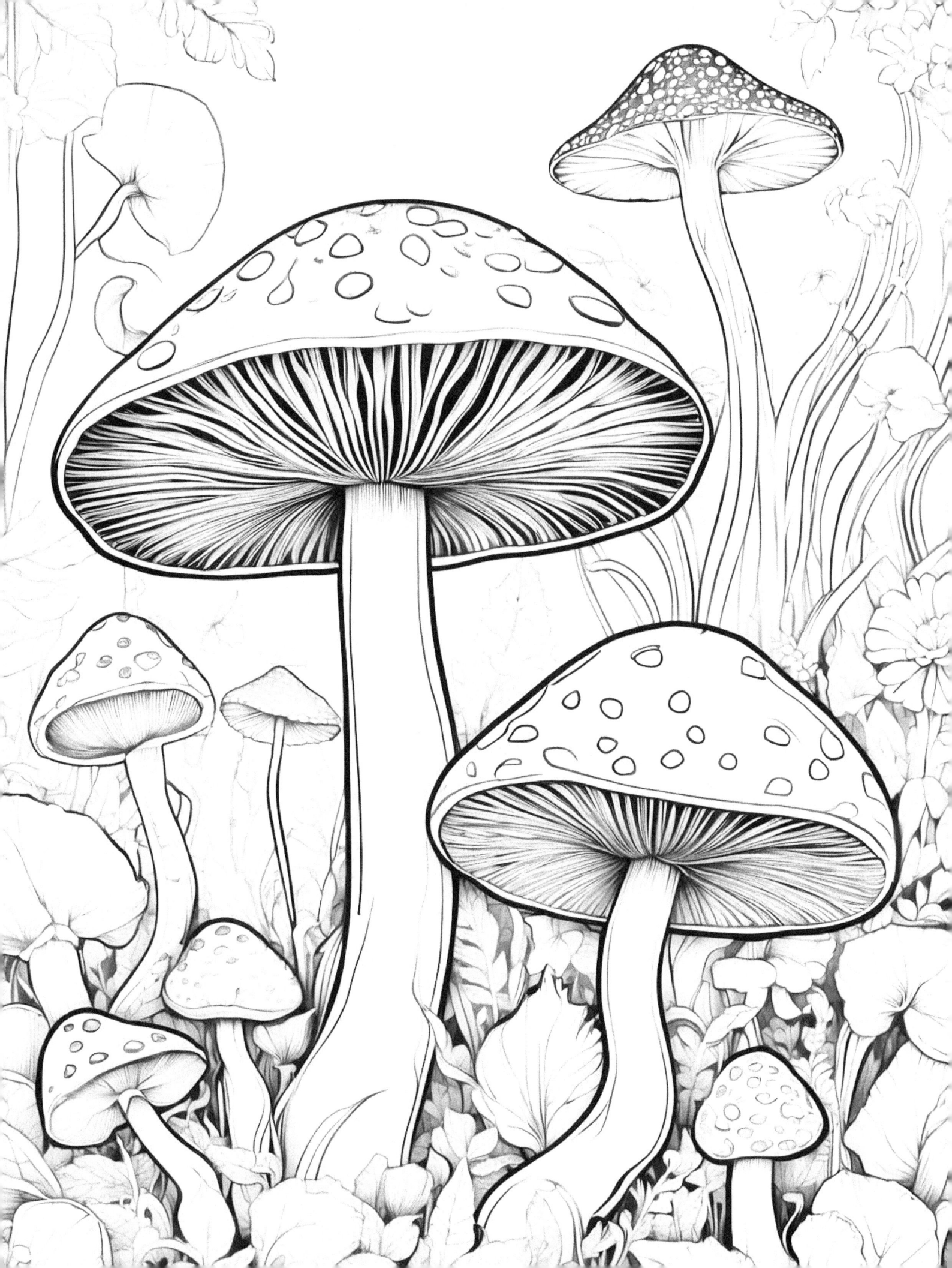

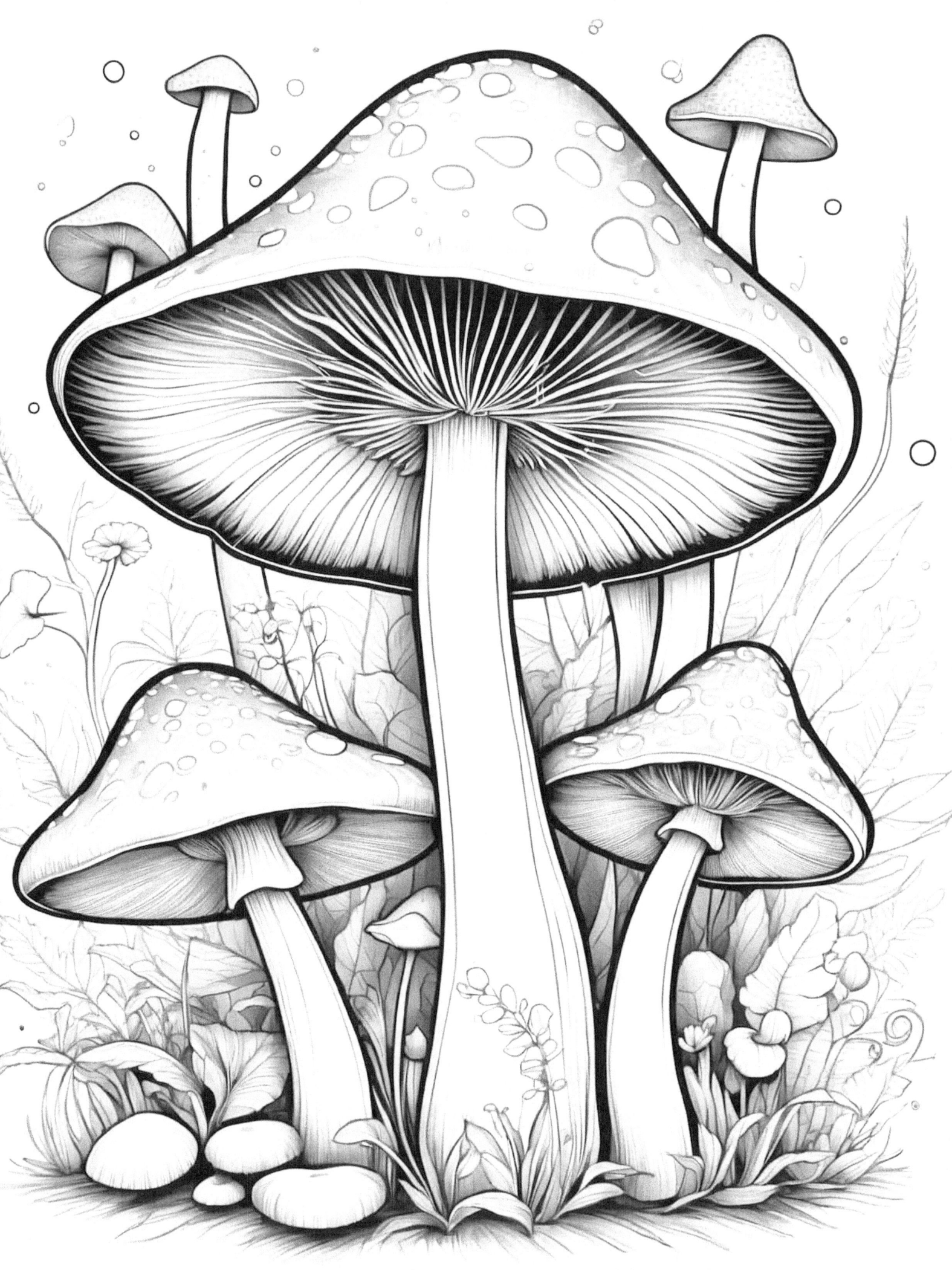

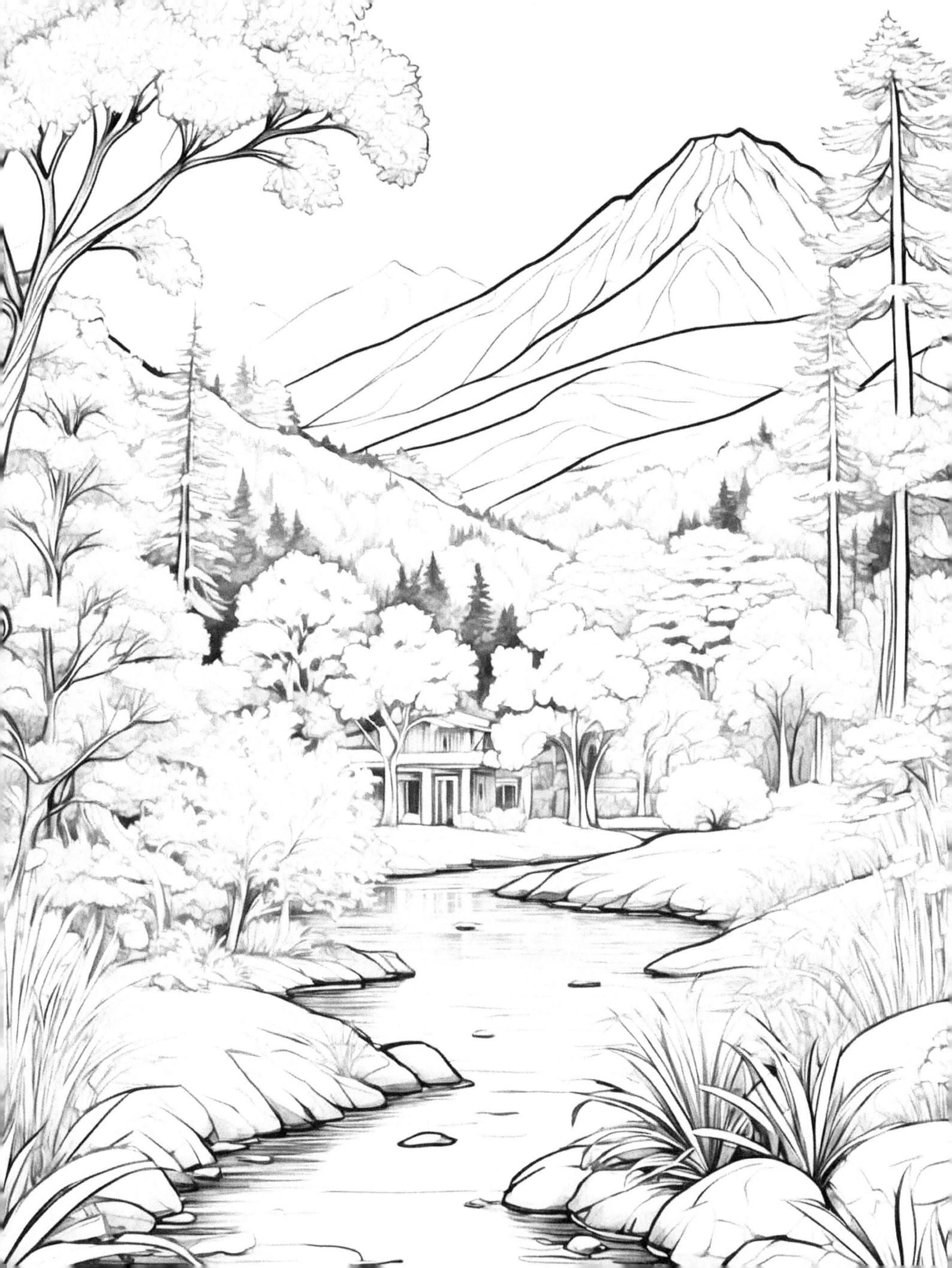

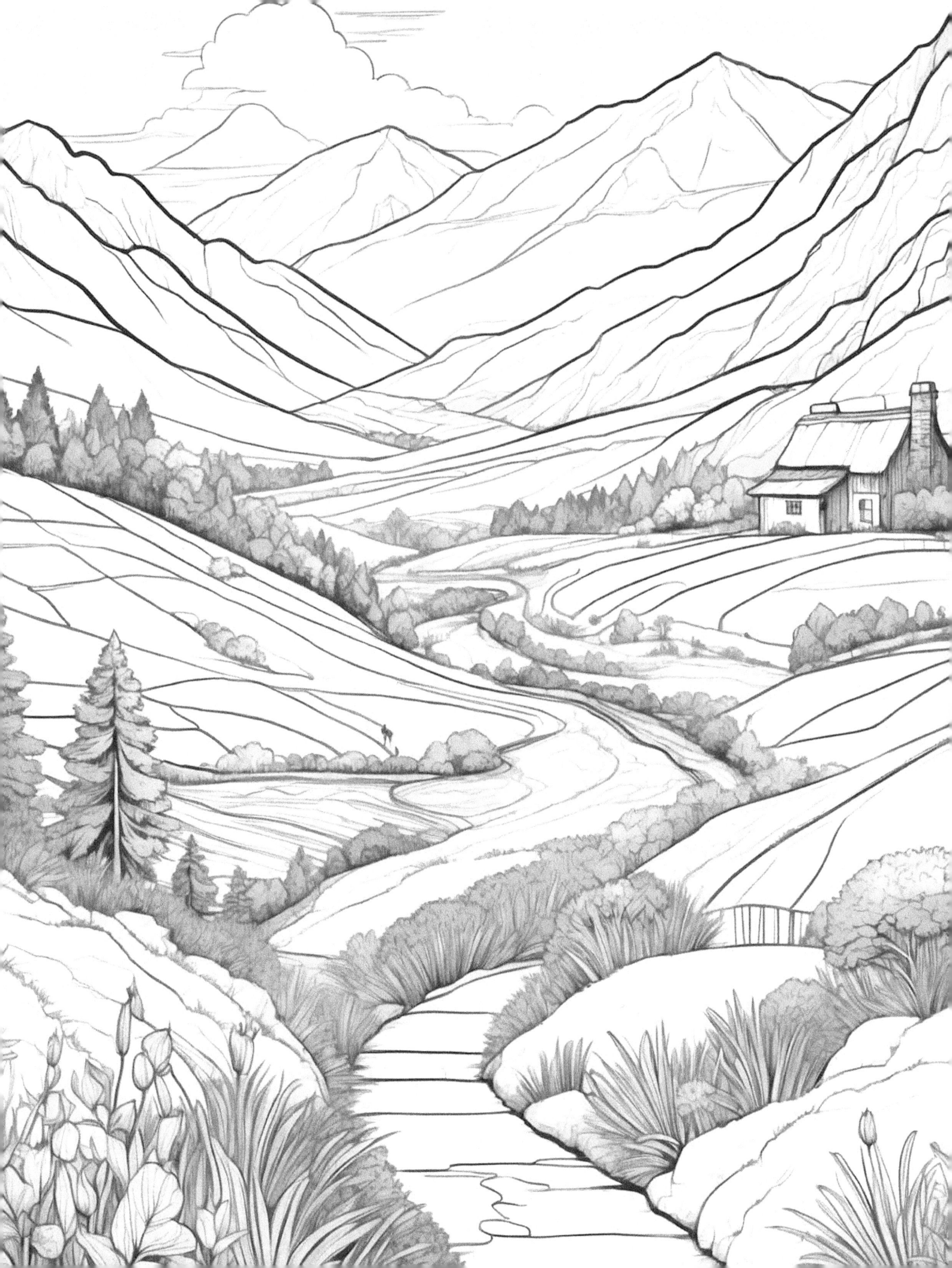

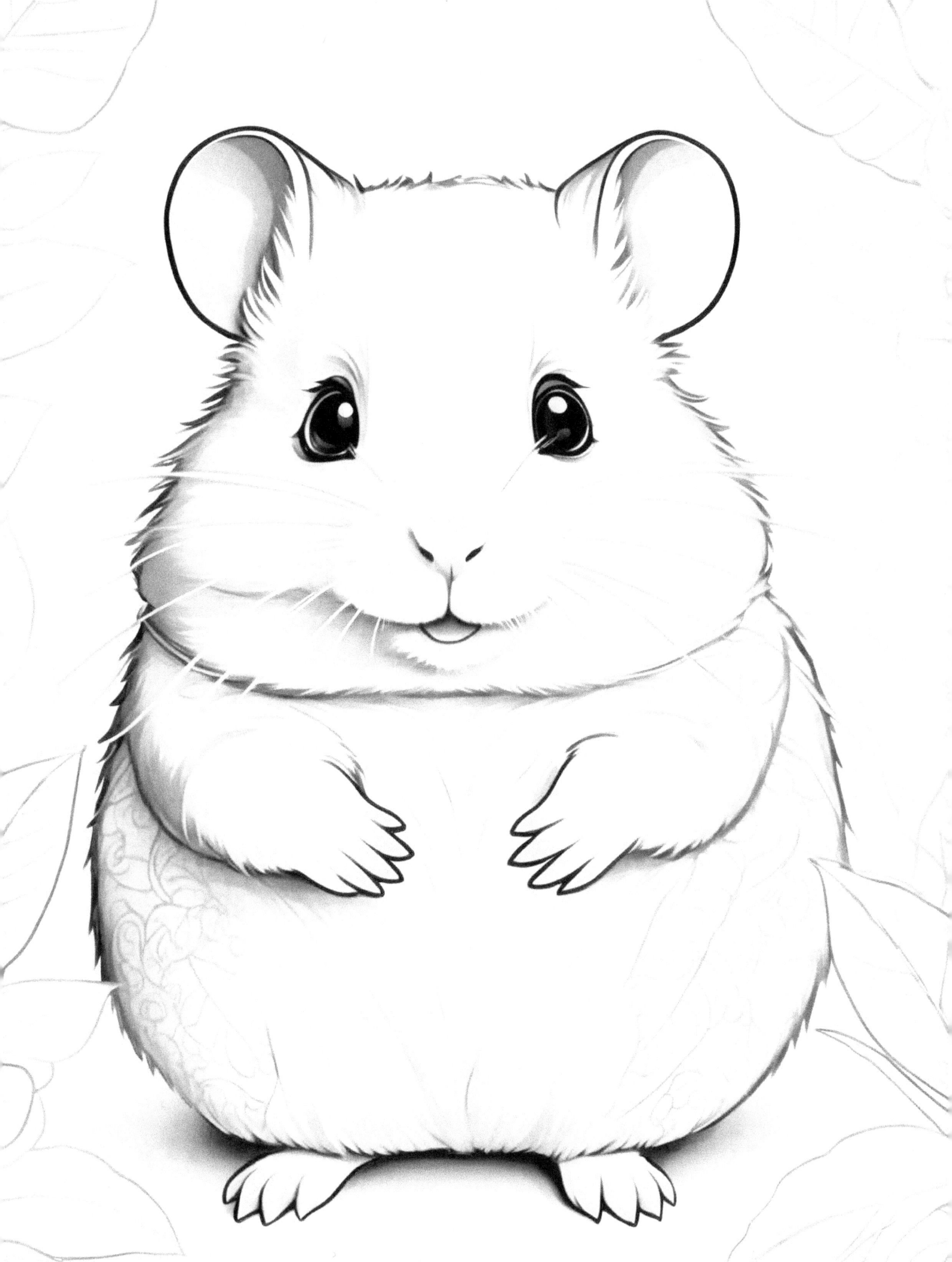

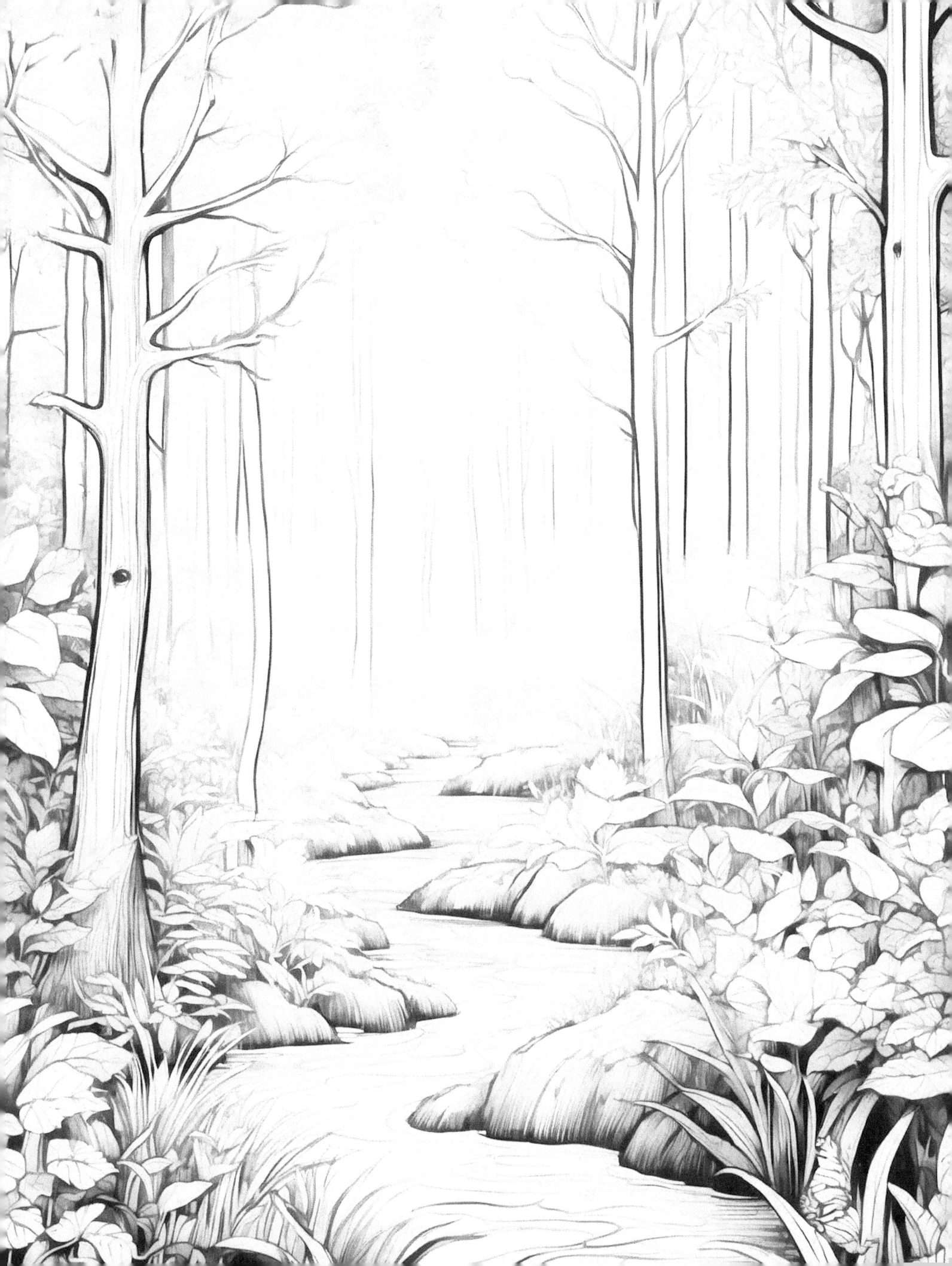

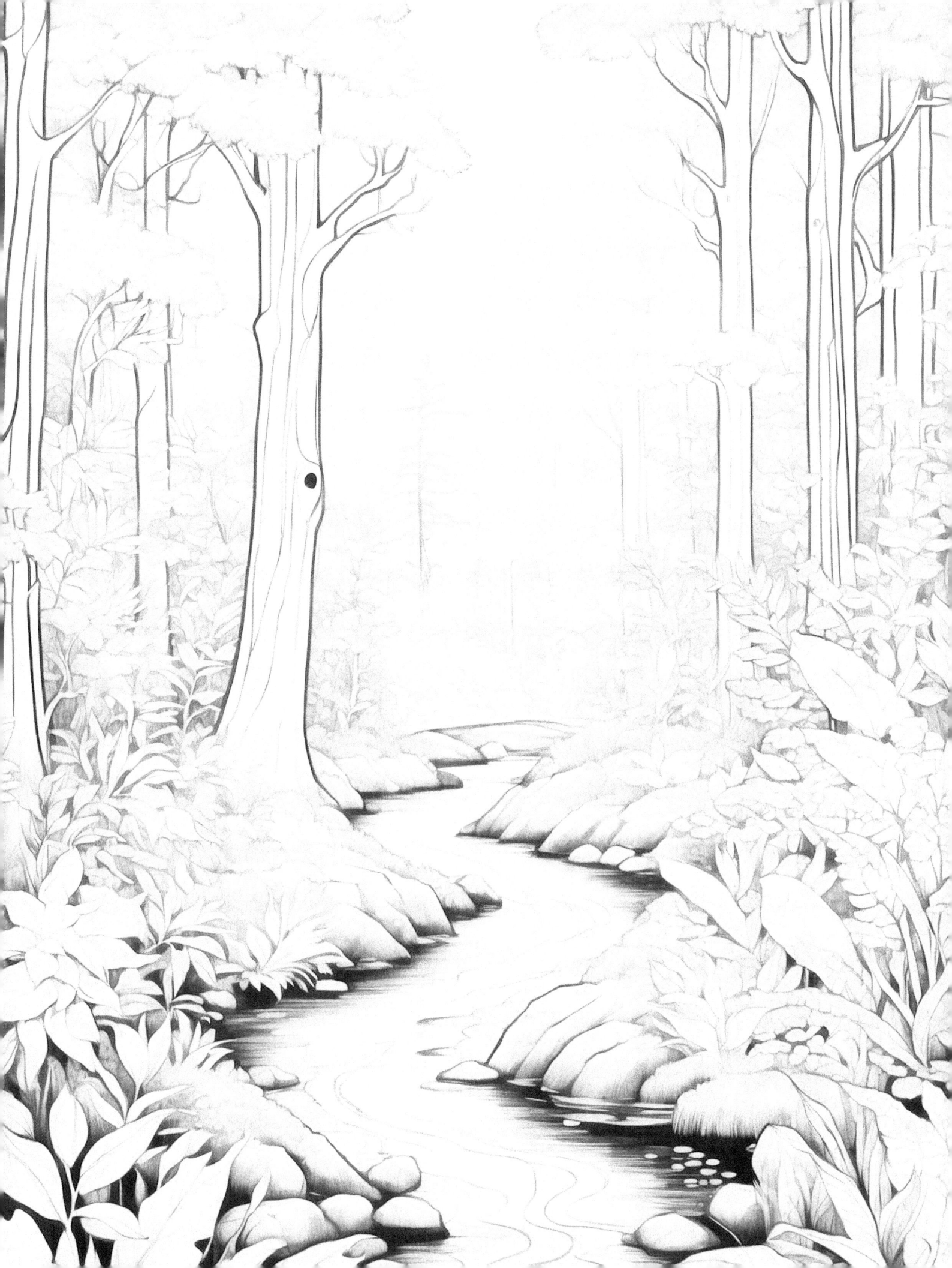

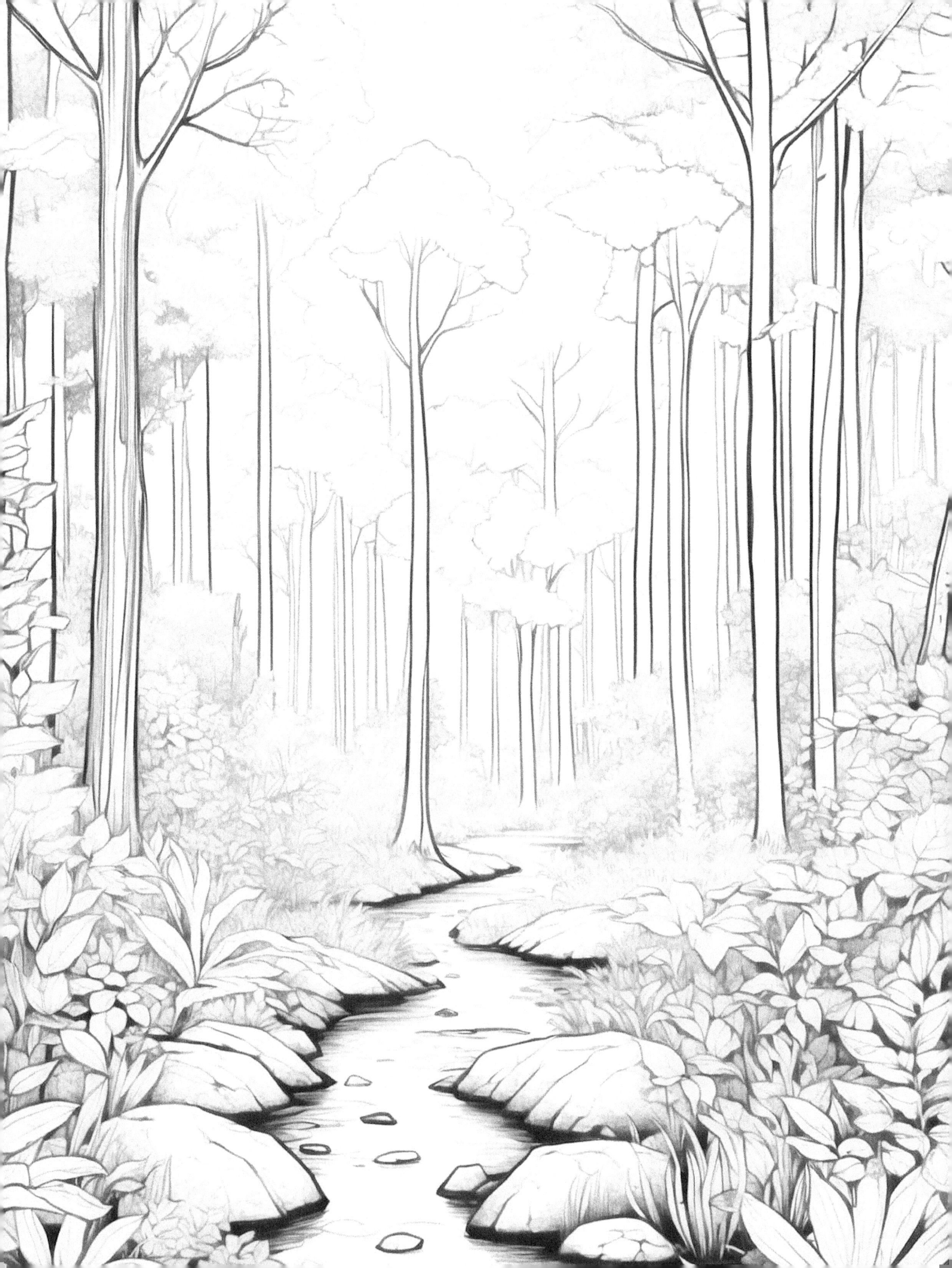

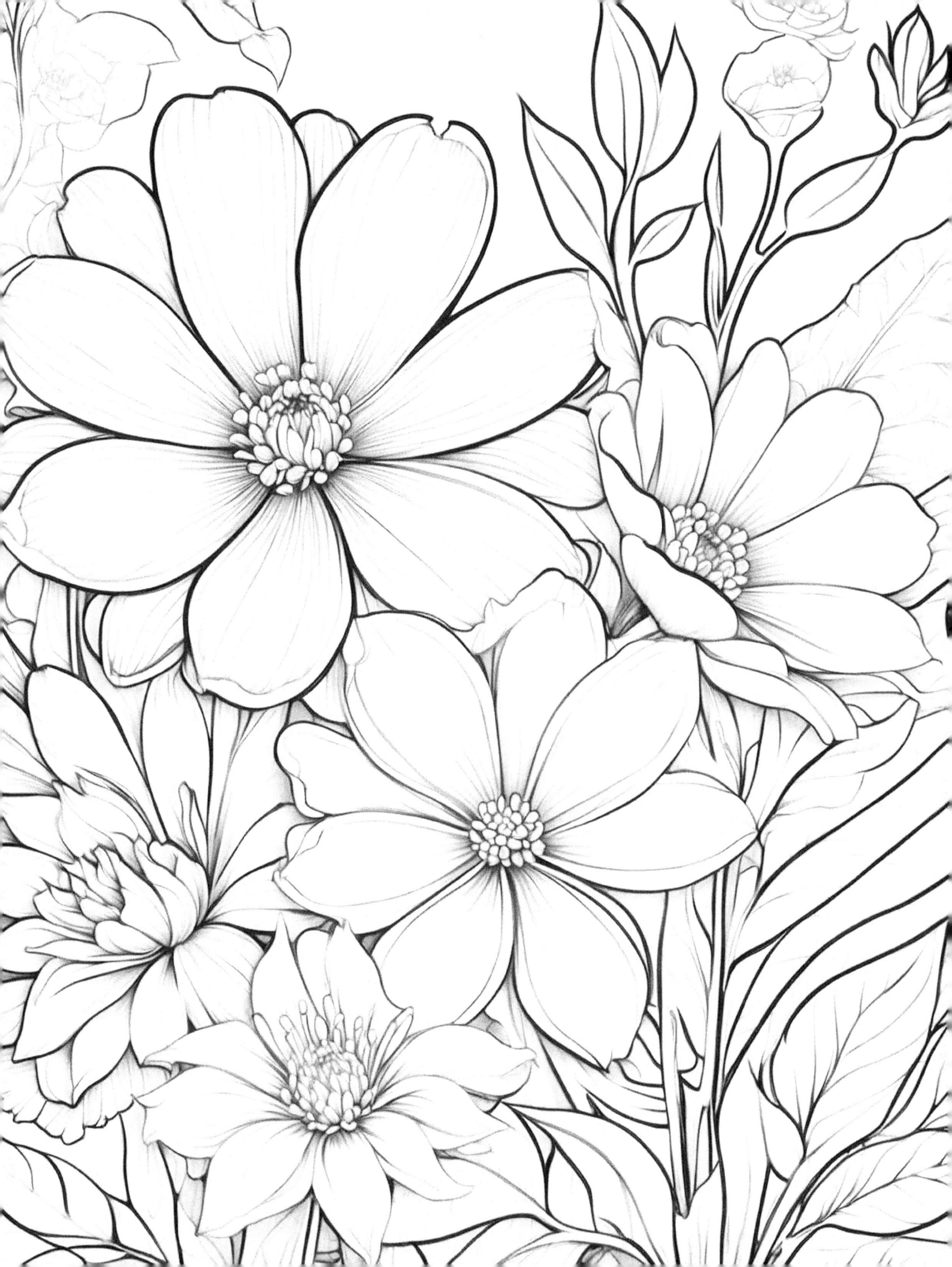

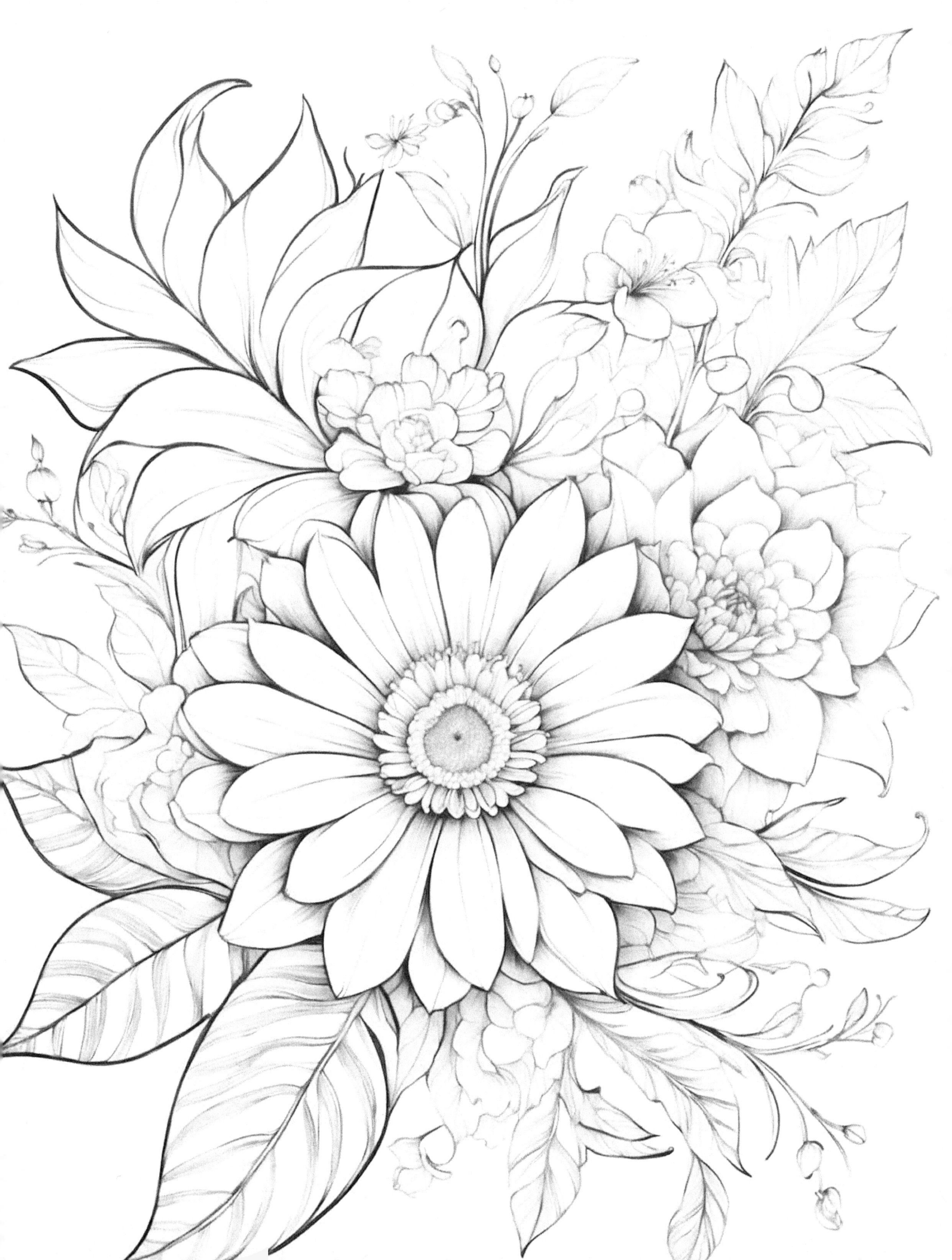

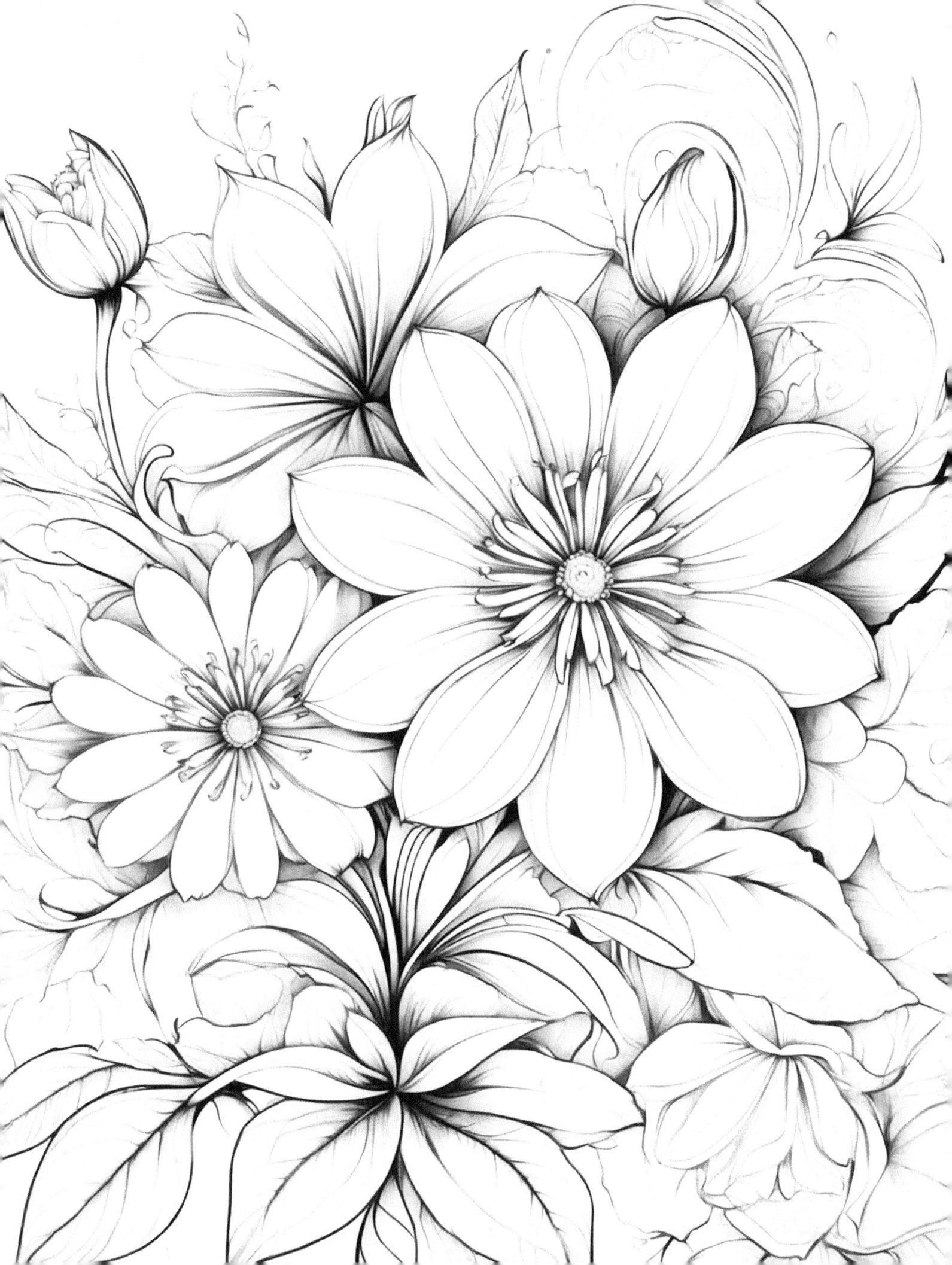

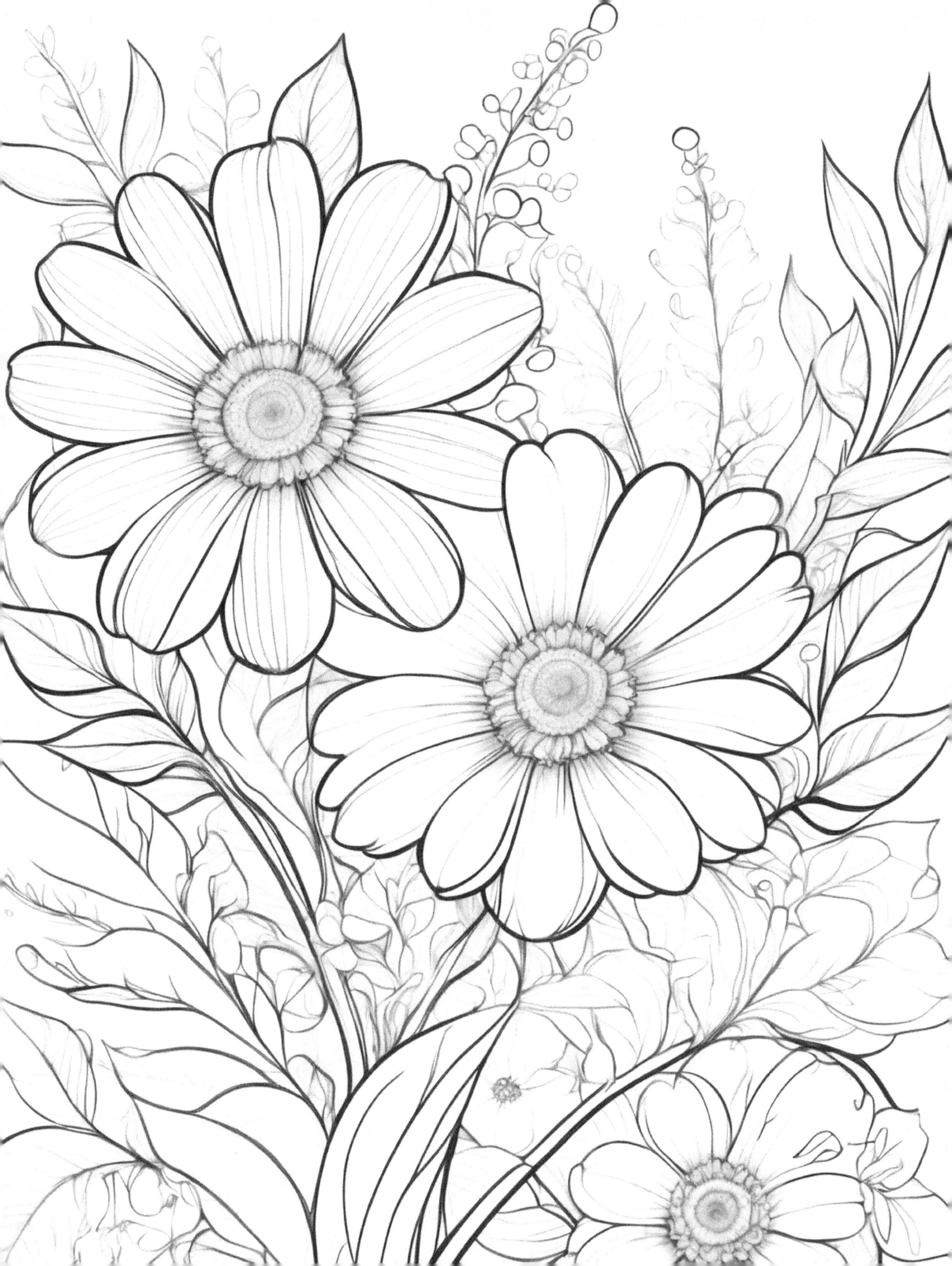

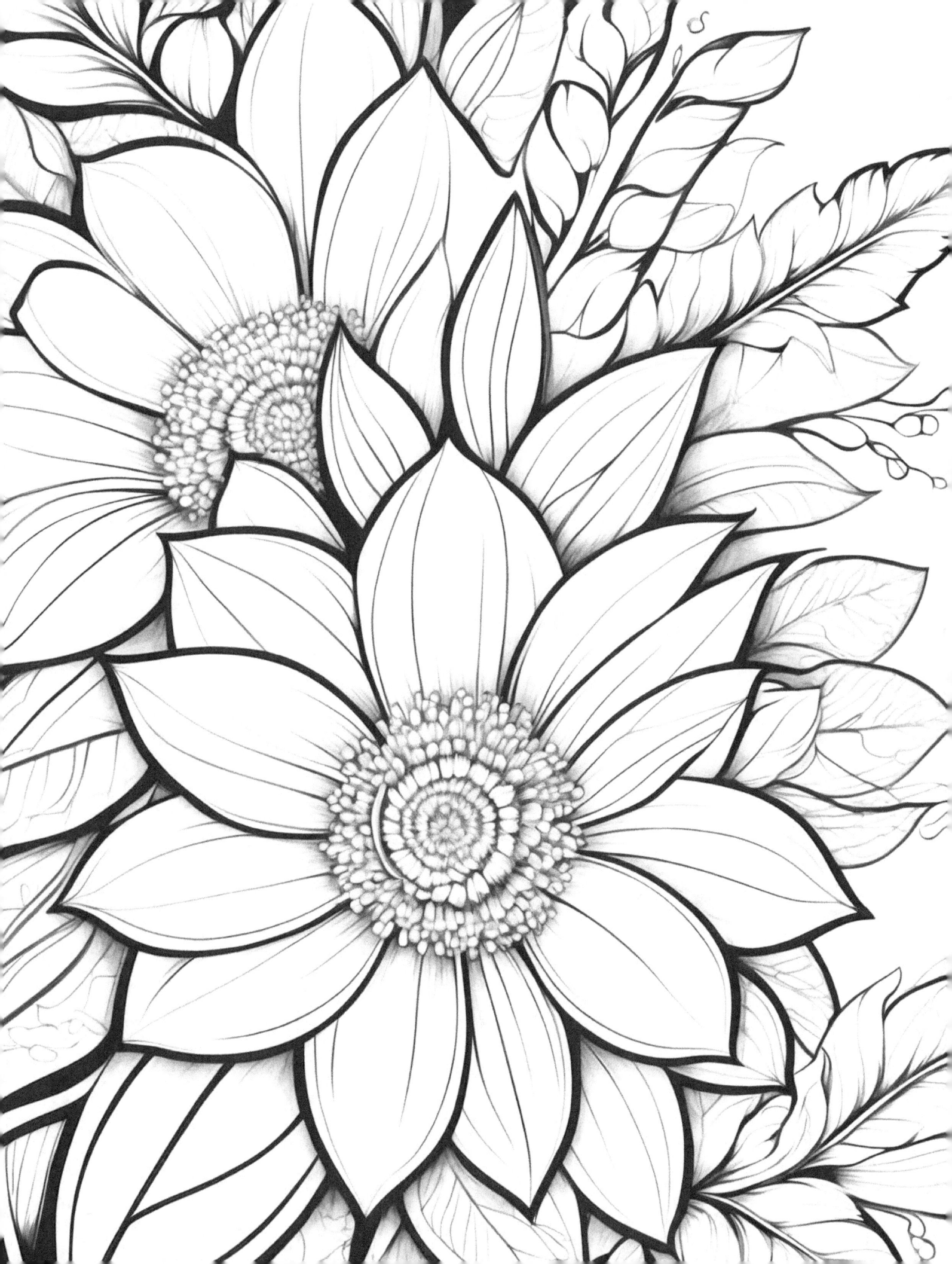

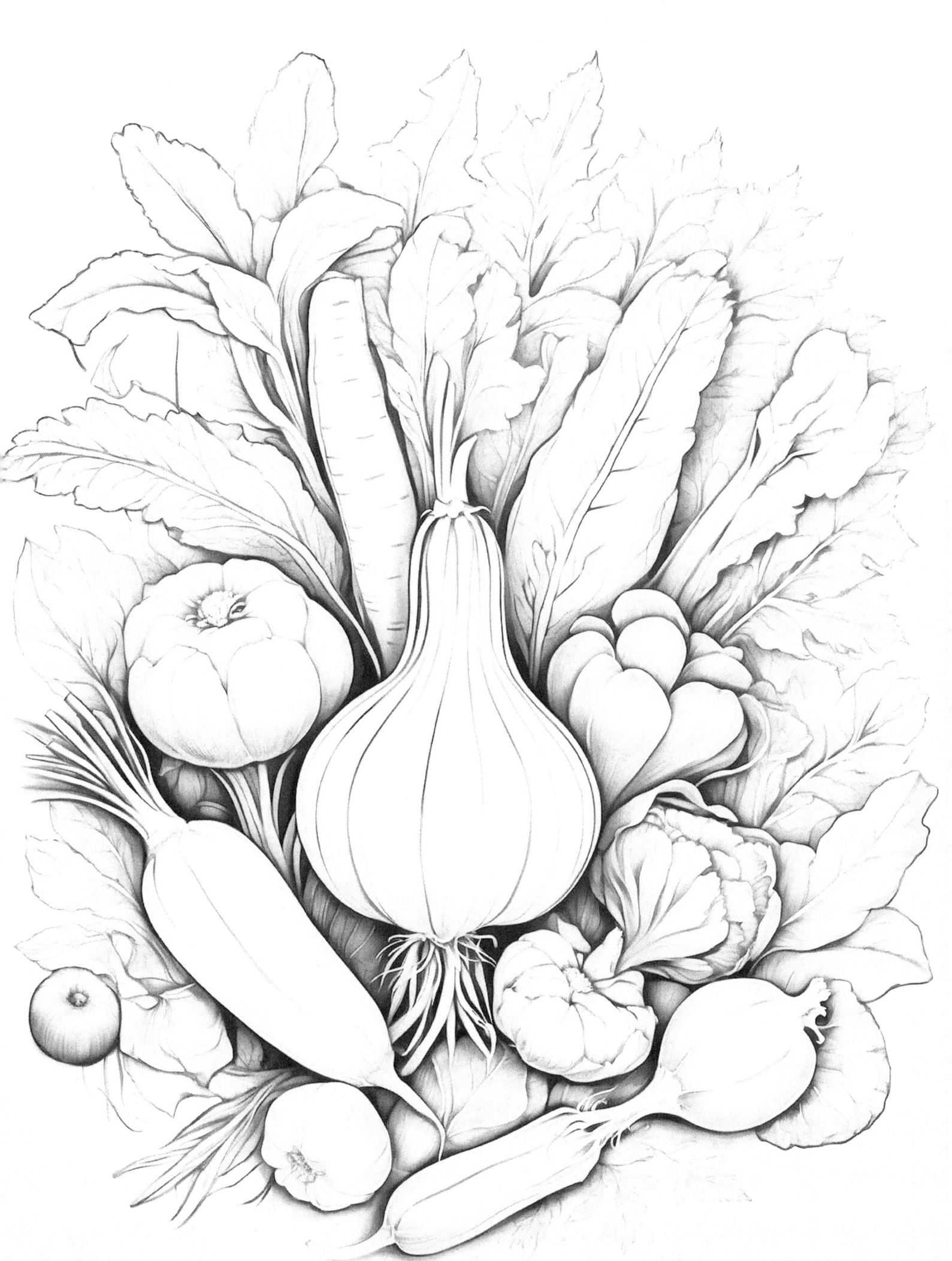

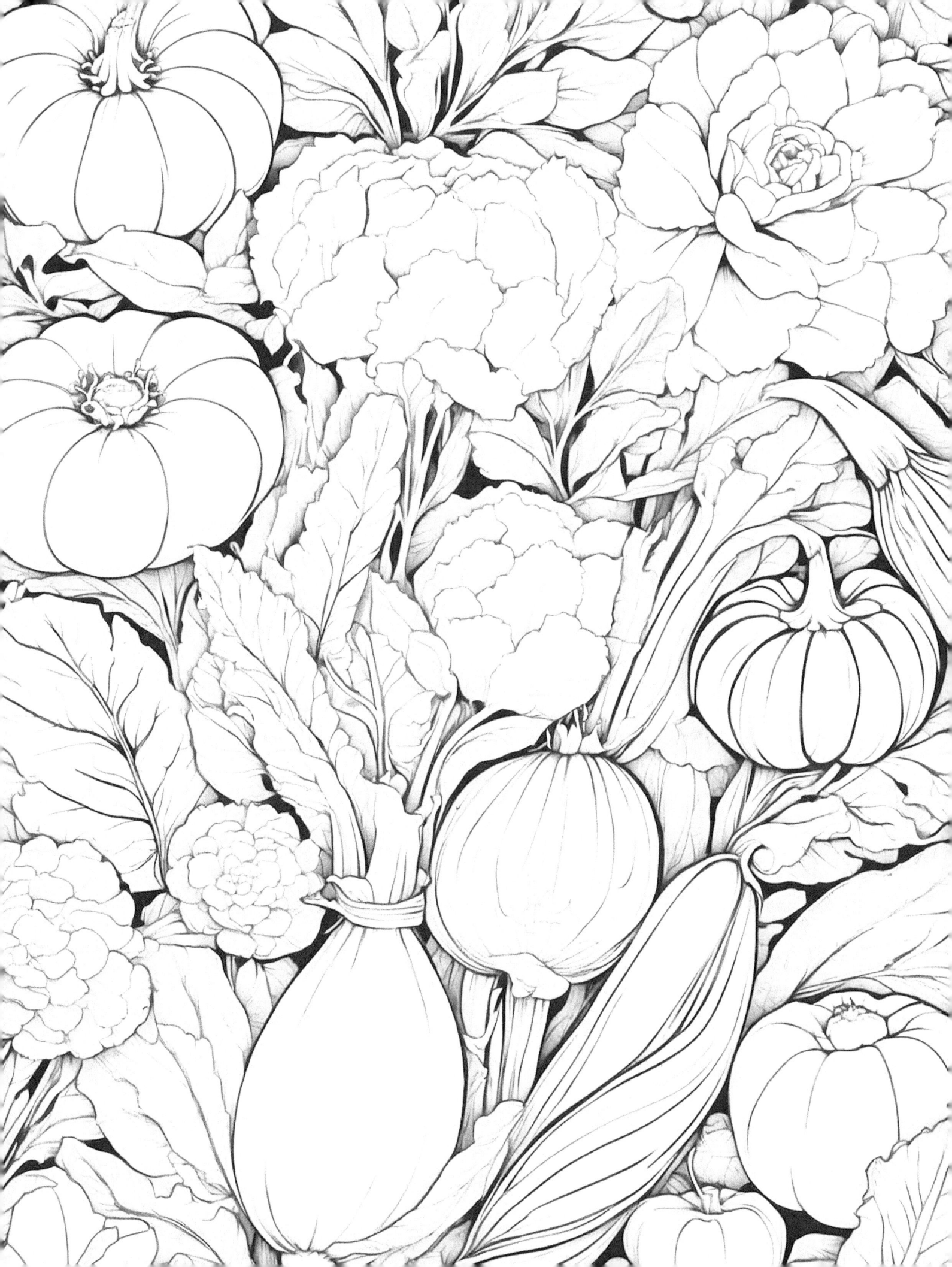

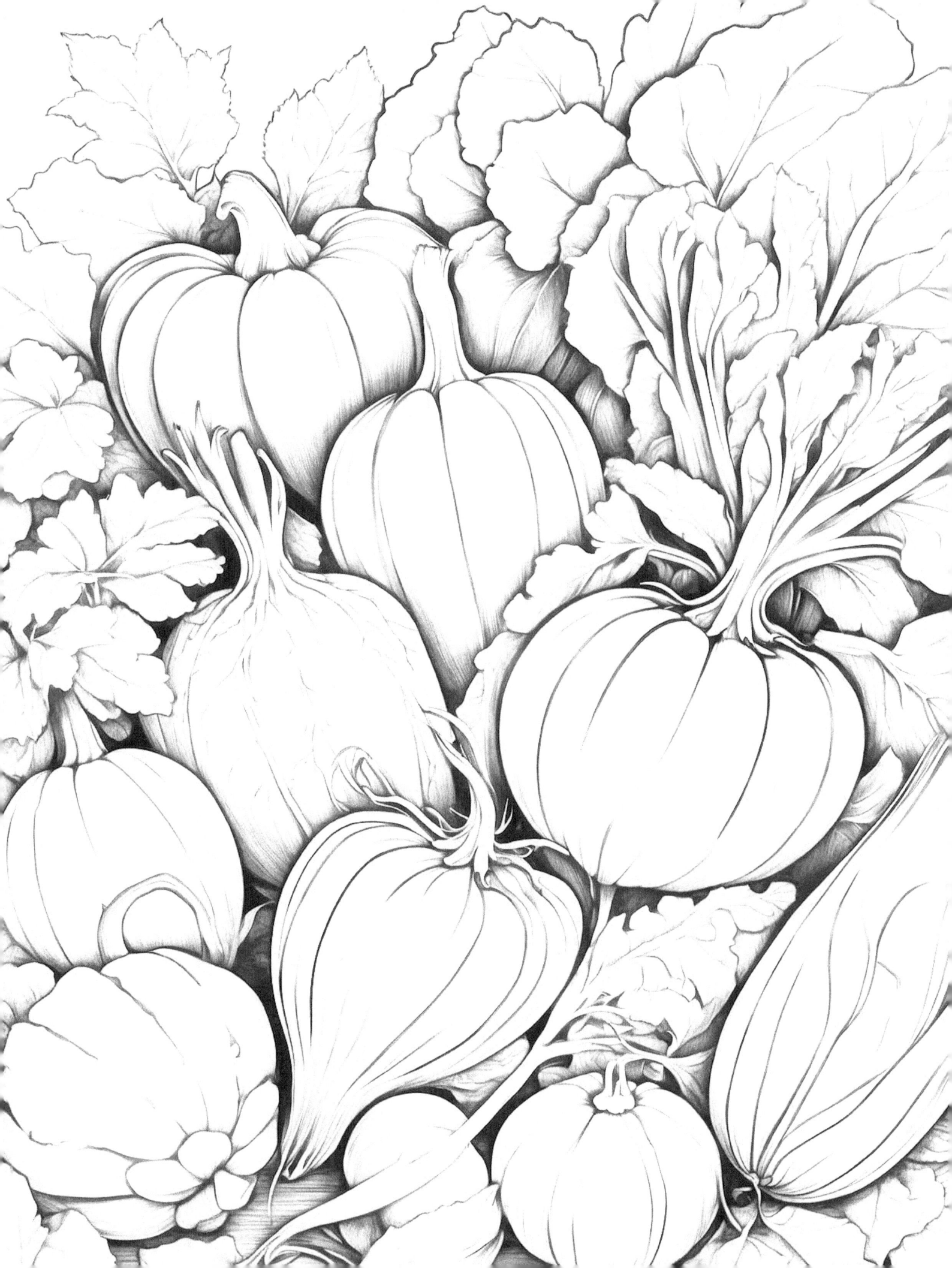

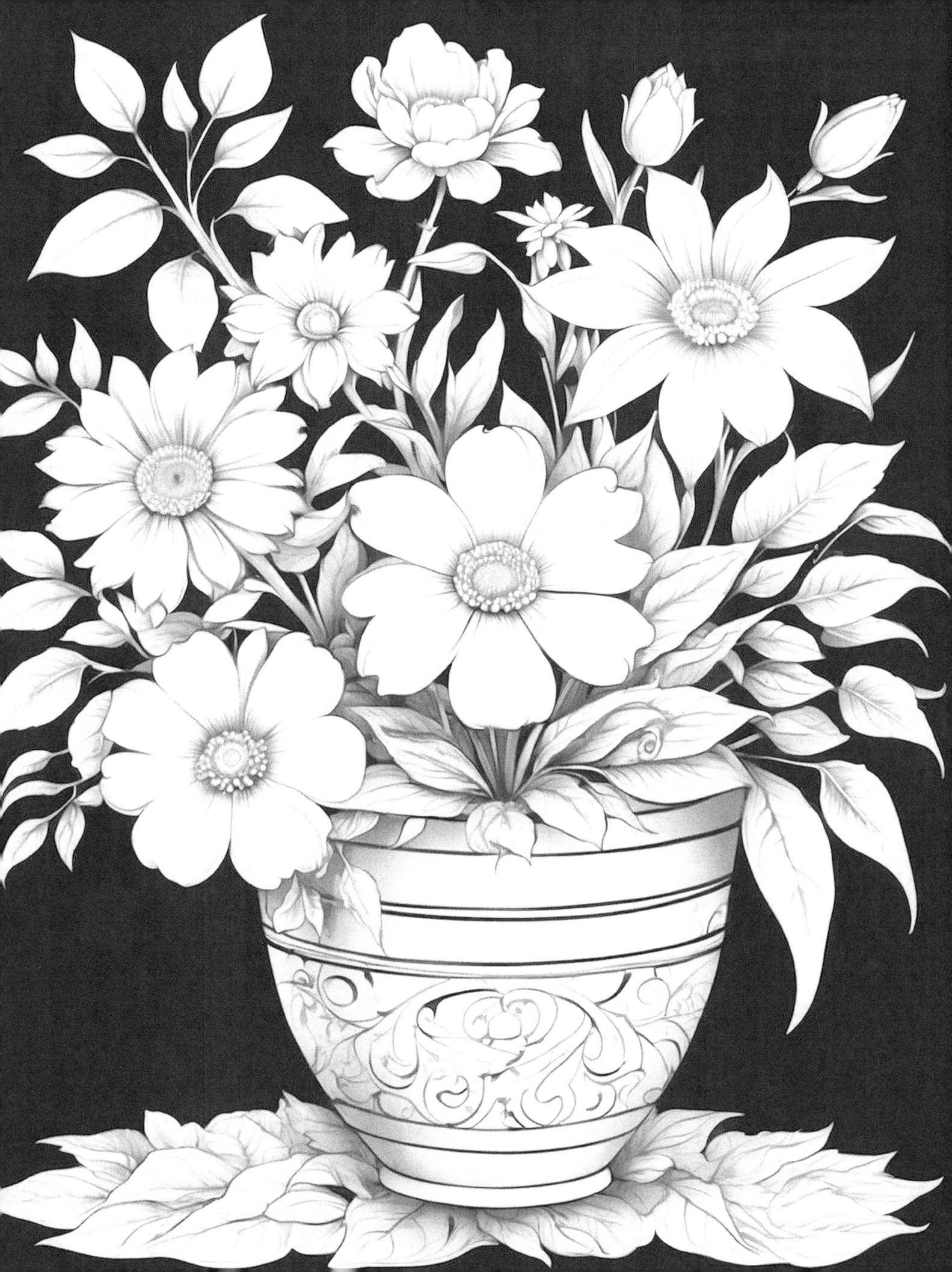

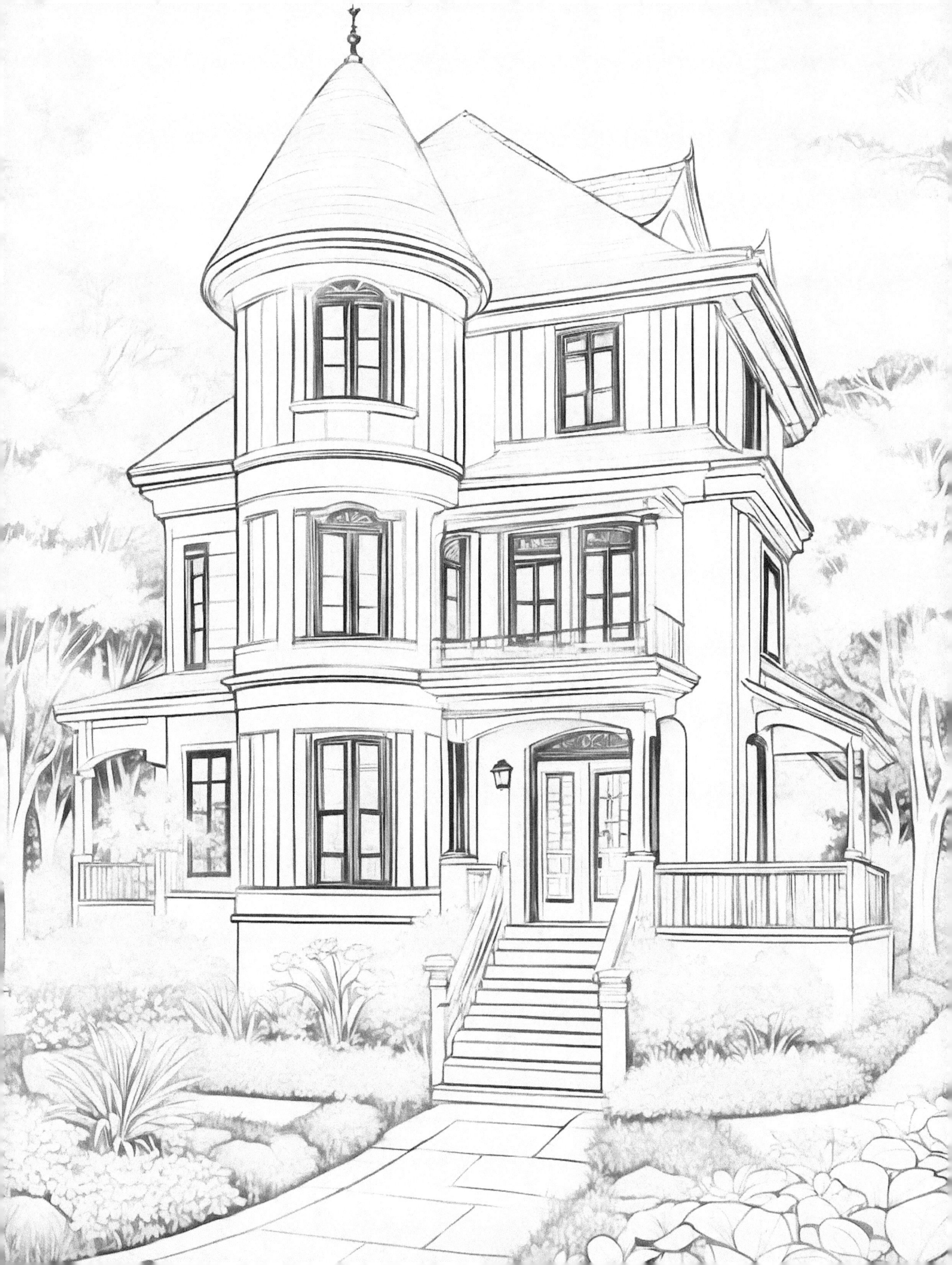

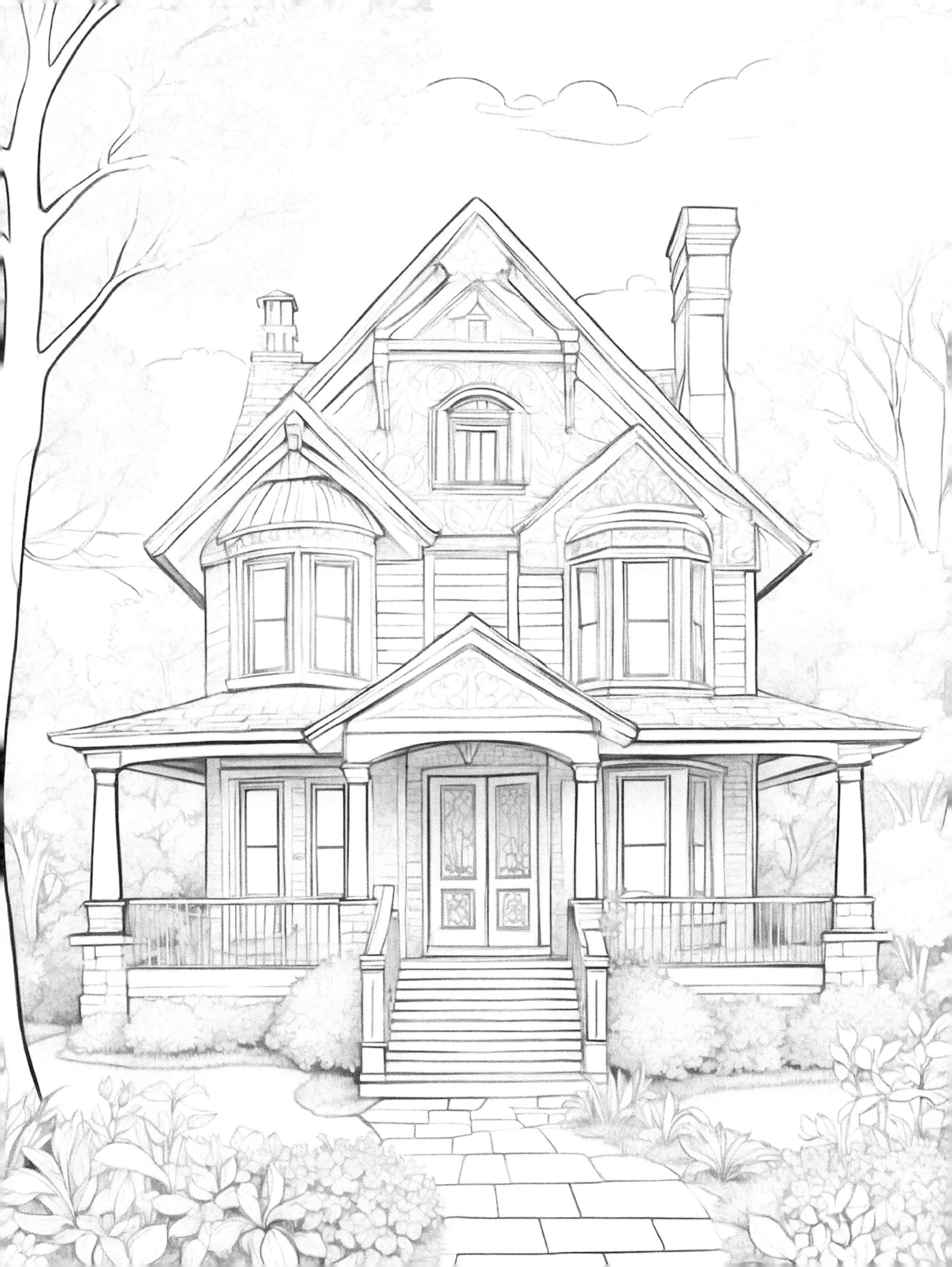

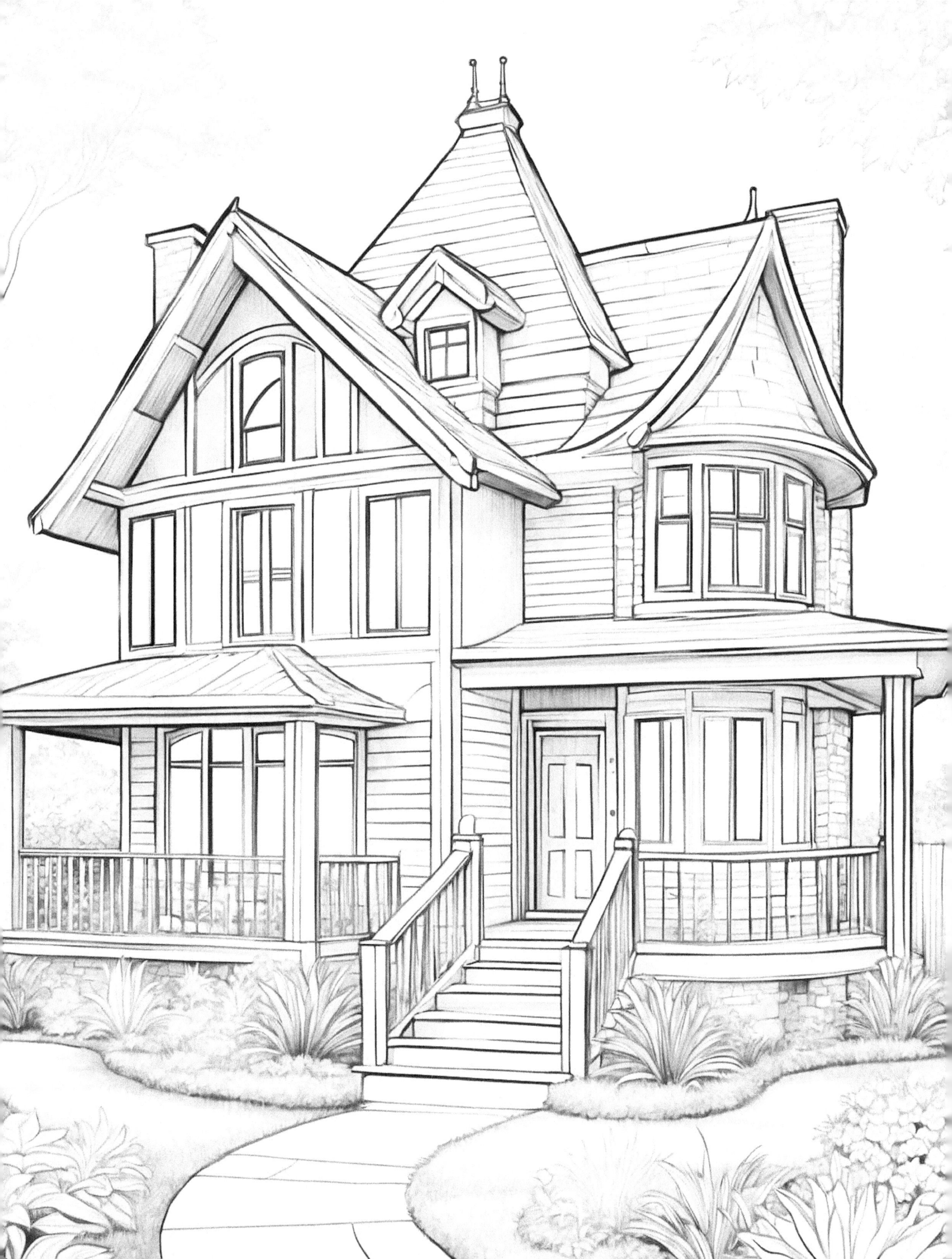

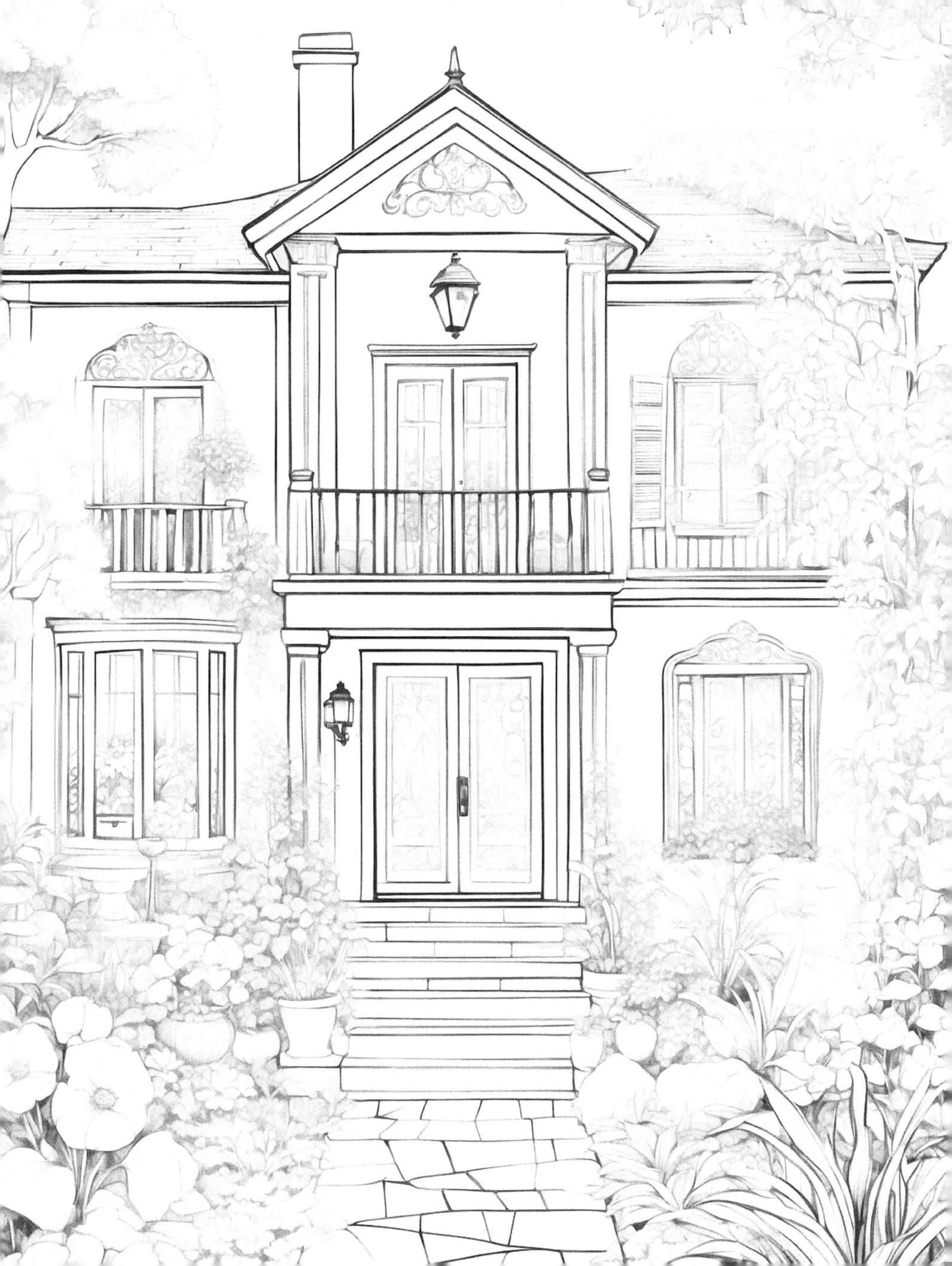

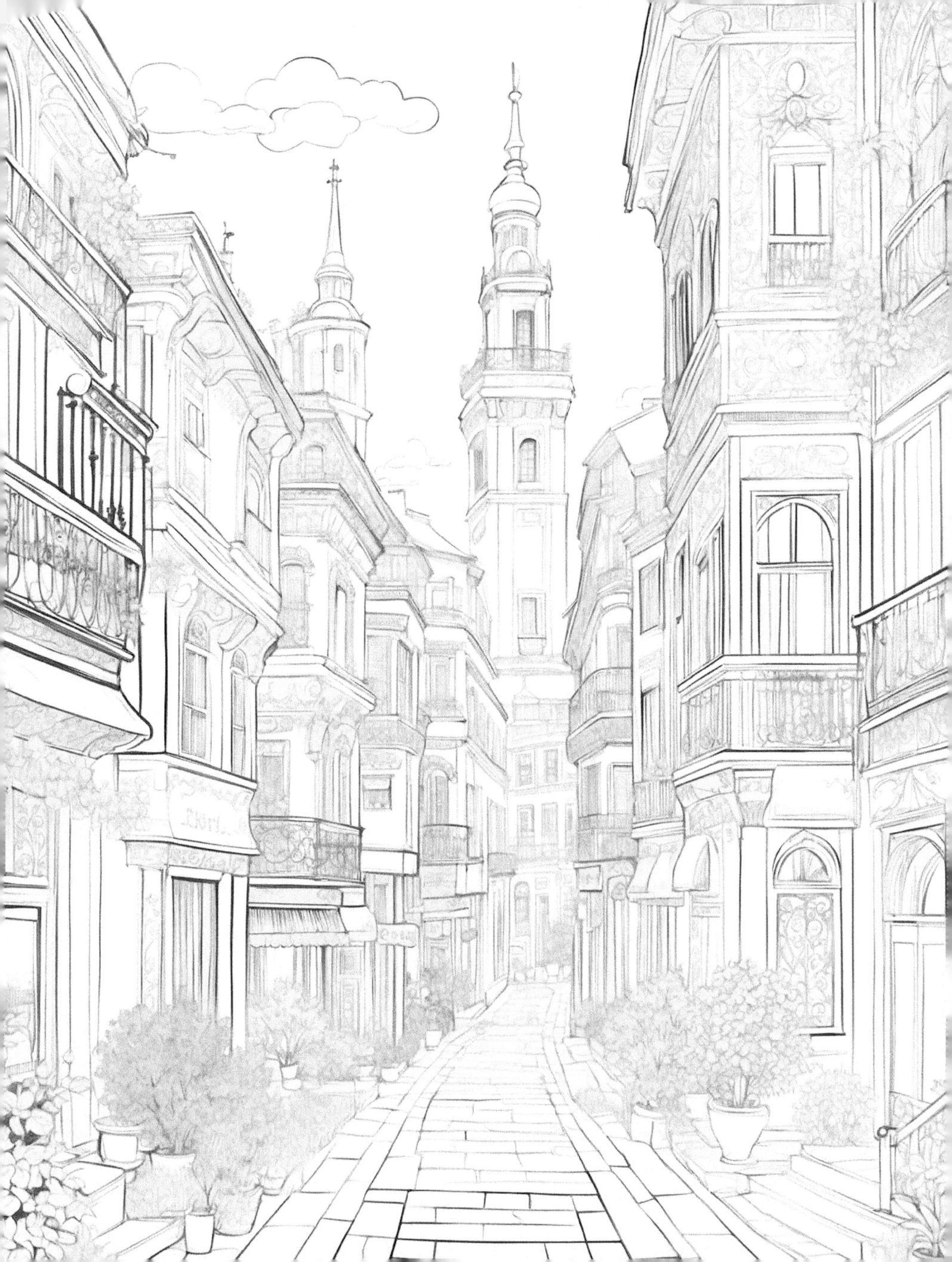

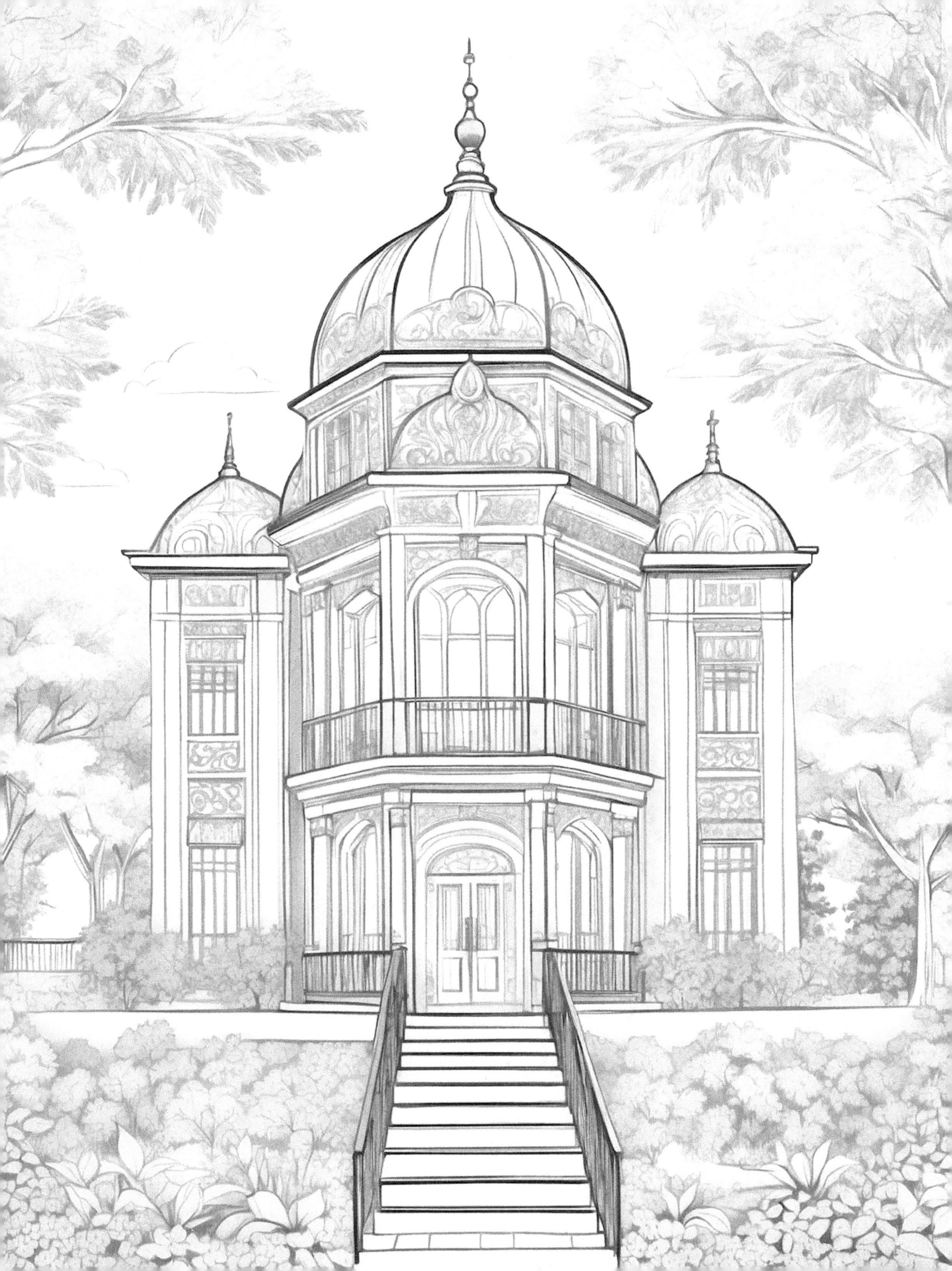

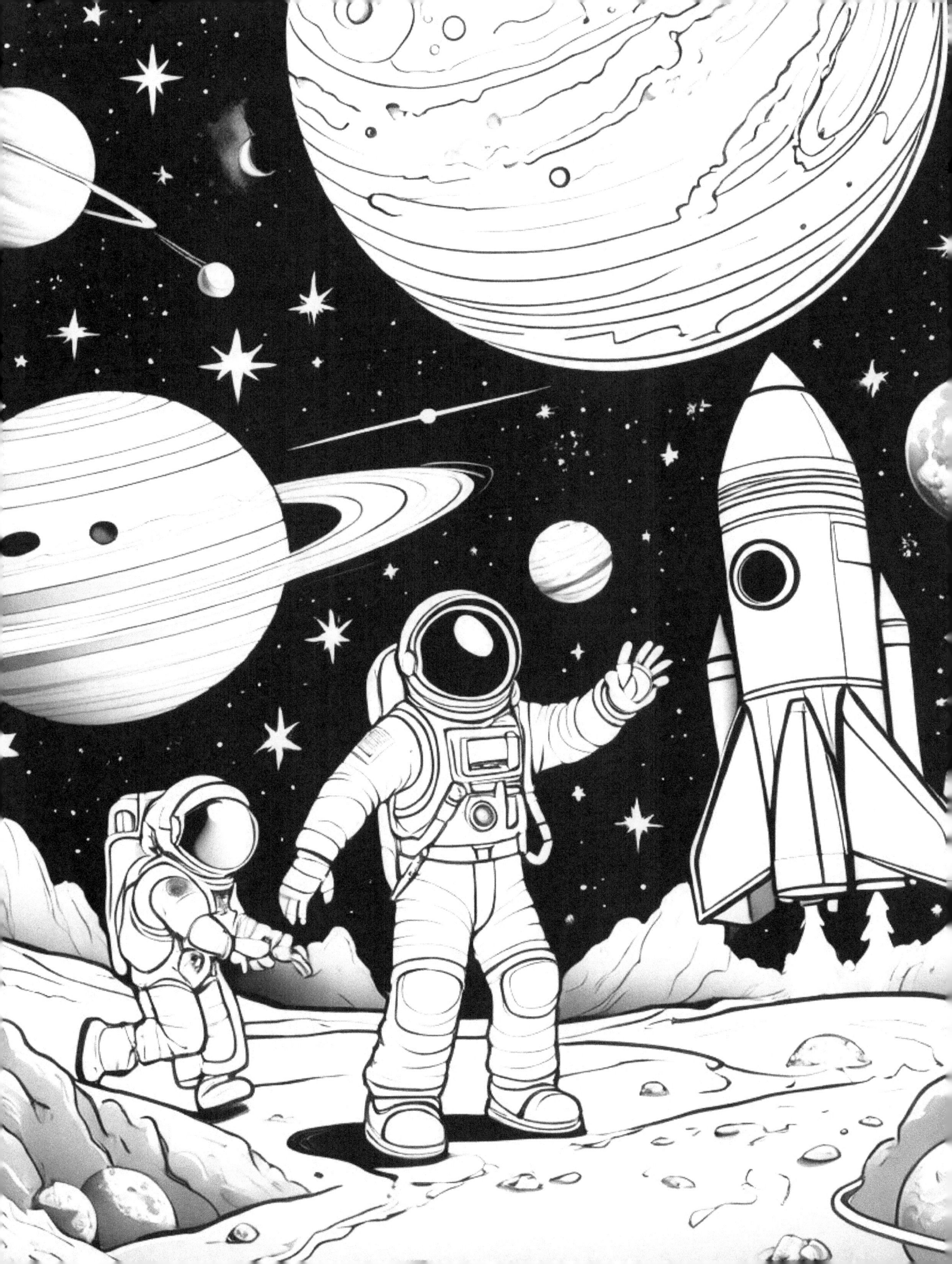

www.ingramcontent.com/pod-product-compliance
Lightning Source LLC
Chambersburg PA
CBHW062355220526
45472CB00008B/1817